The Rise of the Cobot

The Rise of the Cobot

Grow Your Business Exponentially with Collaborative Artificial Intelligence

John Rauscher and Matt Rauscher

ISBN: 978-2-9567951-4-8

Graphs include pictures designed by Freepik and Smashicons from Flaticon.

Backgrounds are from Unsplash.

Showeet designed the graphs in chapters 4 and 6.

Contents

Introduction

Every day, articles, blogs, and interviews are published on the subject of artificial intelligence (AI). For some experts, like Luc Julia, cocreator of Siri and vice president of innovation at Samsung, AI does not exist. For many others, AI is a technological marvel with capabilities that will soon exceed those of humans in many areas. Whom should we believe? For most of the hundreds of business leaders and executives interviewed for this book, the concrete uses of AI are an enigma. In fact, AI is already a part of our daily lives, but few of us recognize the added value this new technology can bring to our businesses, especially those in the service sector. This lack of understanding is powered by a collective imagination that projects as many hopes as it does fears on AI. In this book, you will discover a new positive and realistic vision of AI, brought to life by business experience in deploying AI projects: collaborative artificial intelligence, where the value of AI comes from the collaboration between humans and AI. In this book, when we speak about AI, we refer to the artificial intelligence technology. And when we say collaborative AI, we mean the collaborative approach where humans and AI work together to achieve a goal.

The term *artificial intelligence* has existed for more than sixty years. Computer pioneers like Alan Turing, Marvin Minsky, and John McCarthy, to name a few, had anticipated that computers would become machines capable of mimicking certain aspects of human intelligence. We will rely on Marvin Minsky's definition of AI: "the science of making machines do things that would require intelligence if done by men." Considerable progress has been made these past sixty years, as researchers and computer scientists strive to build computers capable of mimicking the human brain.

AI covers many technologies, but the general public knows of only two of them: machine learning (ML), which is self-learning by computers, and deep learning, which is the most advanced version. Google, Amazon, Facebook, and Apple (GAFA) are betting on the latest ML technology to meet the internal analysis needs of their gigantic collected databases and targeted advertising. In this book, we go beyond self-learning because other lesser-known AI technologies, among them those related to human language, are revolutionizing service activities and providing invaluable gains in both work quality and efficiency.

Well before the current wave of media coverage, AI-based automation was already successfully adopted by some business sectors. For example, industrial production companies have been using it for the past forty years. First-generation AI, such as Expert systems, with computer programs that emulate human decision-making through lists of rules, has been involved in many repetitive processes and activity management since the 1980s. As a result, factories gradually started producing manufactured goods with an increased level of precision, reliability, quality, and productivity. This automation and AI-driven shift in manufacturing has greatly improved, in a matter of decades, the quality of manufactured goods, such as televisions, telephones, and cars, all the while significantly decreasing their prices.

What This Means for Your Business

This book addresses AI applications for business service activities regardless of sector or size. You will learn how your company can become the leader in its local, national, international, business-to-business (B2B), or business-to-consumer (B2C) market by deploying collaborative AI. From an entrepreneur's point of view, rather than that of a computer scientist, we will discuss deep business, rather than deep technology, using simplified language aimed at the general public regardless of computer knowledge.

Collaboration between AI and humans paves the way to a new generation of high-quality services based on AI that were unthinkable just a few years ago. It will shake up the business model of companies whose core business is the sale of intellectual services: individualized advice to each customer will be dematerialized, much like the internet dematerialized information these past thirty years or so. The word dematerialization might often suggest no cost in the medium term. However, we will explain why this upheaval is a great opportunity for all companies in the service sector and their workers, even those selling reasoning-based services. For companies whose model is the sale of services that require equipment (cleaning, public works, etc.) or the production and marketing of physical products, collaborative AI represents a major business model advancement, one that allows premium positioning where price is no longer the predominant deciding factor as it is in the low-cost sector.

The first chapter of this book covers the major concepts behind the emergence of collaborative AI. In the following three chapters, we define the three main influences of AI for all companies:

1. The automation of repetitive tasks, which enables employees to focus on value-added tasks and create new products and services.
2. Collaborative robots (cobots) that will revolutionize the nature of daily work and allow less-qualified employees to find a role in a company.
3. The modern marketing augmented by AI that will radically change the way companies market and sell a product or service, allowing for premium positioning.

Each chapter is illustrated with concrete and specific examples, whether related to marketing, sales, customer service, consulting, or any other reasoning-based service activity. Our hope is that you will be inspired by these real-life examples to fuel an AI deployment strategy in your company.

Chapter 5 features our analysis of AI's social consequences, the future of recruitment, and why AI creates jobs for all those who want to work regardless of their skill level.

In chapter 6, we share the seven keys to a great AI project so that your first initiative is a success. Chapter 7 explains possible choices and provides the basic technical knowledge needed before developing an AI project. Finally, in chapter 8 we offer a vision of AI's near future, with important insights and predictions that will accelerate its deployment in companies in the short term. We have ignored science fiction because what really matters today is to get started with *available* AI, not to dream.

This book is based on our field experience as entrepreneurs. Since 2010, we have participated in the deployment of dozens of AI projects for hundreds of thousands of users. These experiences have confirmed the magnitude of the current AI revolution and its varied application fields for all companies, large and small. We never witnessed any layoffs at the companies we followed, who told us of growth increases at rates they'd never seen before. We are respecting these clients' anonymity, as they do not wish to reveal their leadership "secret weapon." Some even avoid talking about AI or cobots internally for fear of causing unwarranted misgivings. However, all the examples mentioned in this book are actual use cases deployed in companies.

A real services revolution is underway, and your competitors both in the United States and overseas are embarking on a massive adoption of AI. It is both critical and urgent that you act now, not only to keep them from infringing on your market share but also to help you gain additional shares and become a market leader.

If you are a CEO or an executive in a company with service activities, a management committee member, a top administrator, or a department head and you want to understand concretely how to make the most of today's available AI without lessening your human and societal responsibility, then this book is for you. You will discover which strategy to put in place in the pages that follow.

1.

Collaborative Artificial Intelligence

Nothing will be less industrial than the civilization that comes from the Industrial Revolution.

Jean Fourastié[1]

1 *Jean Fourastié is the author of The Great Hope of the Twentieth Century, first published in French in Paris in 1949.*

Although artificial intelligence (AI) has been around for decades, it has experienced a true renaissance in recent years. This renewed interest can be explained first of all by the technological progress enjoyed by two major pillars of modern AI: machine learning, which is also known as ML (the set of learning technologies that allows the machine to generate reasoning algorithms by itself), and computer language management (language understanding, language generation, intelligent dialogue, and translation). The success of these technologies has been driven mainly by the growth of cheap, reliable, and fast cloud computing, allowing users to share powerful servers and access large databases. Data and fast computing powers AI technology. AI solutions, once only available to scientific laboratories and large corporations, are now affordable and available to all who possess a minimum of technological expertise.

The service sector has undergone many changes since the advent of the internet in the 1990s, and AI promises to be a new and decisive stage in its history. Let's take a closer look at the milestones that have marked this sector's evolution.

First, there were Services 1.0, namely traditional services, such as in-store sales, catalog sales, or telephone support. Then came Services 2.0, which correspond to the internet dematerialization of services that invite users to give their opinion, as in e-commerce, and therefore allow the sharing of knowledge and experience. Consumers' aspirations and practices have evolved from an era of ownership to an era of use. It is in this context that Services 3.0, or the sharing economy, has developed. Consumers can now exchange services among themselves—for example, lease their houses with Airbnb, share their cars with Getaround, or even crowdsource investments through peer-to-peer lending sites like Kickstarter. Today, a new revolution is underway and based on collaborative AI. It corresponds to the application of AI to service activities and the dematerialization of expertise (and therefore advice) made possible by technological progress and collaboration between humans and AI. Of the Eurozone economies' gross domestic product (GDP), 73 percent is based on supplying expertise, advice, and therefore services. That number jumps even higher to 80 percent in the United States.[2] The magnitude of the revolution based on collaborative AI may therefore prove to be as great as the revolution ushered in by the invention of the printing press. This new revolution will radically change our habits and our business models, whether we are individuals, small-to-medium enterprises (SMEs), or midmarket or large companies. Along with this paradigm shift, changes to working conditions will be necessary. Such an upheaval cannot be unilaterally imposed due to the risk of being vehemently rejected. In order to be successful, collaborative AI must be understood as bringing value to all—that is, to employees, business owners, and investors alike.

---

2 *"Structure of the Euro Area Economy," European Central Bank, accessed October 8, 2019, http://www.ecb.europa.eu/mopo/eaec/html/index.en.html.*

It is therefore essential to understand the type of companies and workers who will be the most directly affected by this revolution and the issues they will face. Given all the investment in new technology over the last few decades, many economists have been unable to explain a marked slowdown in productivity. From 1971 until 2004, the trend in the Organisation for Economic Co-operation and Development (OECD) countries was growth in productivity, but from 2004 to the present day, the opposite has been happening: productivity has been decreasing slowly. Interestingly, this trend is worse in the United States and the United Kingdom, countries known to embrace new technology.[3] Is technology driving down productivity? Are employees wasting time on social media? Let's now examine the new structural issues behind this surprising slowdown in labor productivity growth, which makes the advent of collaborative AI all the more needed to revive the economy.

Knowledge Workers

Modern employees are essentially knowledge workers, with the exception of those involved in industrial production units. Management guru Peter Drucker, who coined the term, defines them as those employees and executives who apply theoretical and analytical knowledge in their daily work. On the other hand, Thomas Davenport, an American academic who specialized in knowledge management, describes them as employees who make their living by thinking.

---

3 *Ian Golden, Pantelis Koutroumpis, François Lafond, and Julian Winkler, Oxford Martin School, "Why Is Productivity Slowing Down?," 2018, https://www.oxfordmartin.ox.ac.uk/downloads/academic/Why-is-productivity-slowing-down-WP.pdf*

Whatever definition you use, the term *knowledge worker* was, until recently, only applied to employees with a very high level of education, such as researchers. But this definition was too narrow to describe the evolution of the modern workplace. In the 2000s, it expanded to include not only those with theoretical knowledge but also those who apply any interpretation, sharing, and application of knowledge to a context, no matter how that knowledge was acquired. In other words, employees whose job is to analyze a situation or provide advice are now considered knowledge workers.

The service sector is mostly composed of knowledge workers. They are consultants, lawyers, doctors, salespeople, advisers, architects, computer scientists, and the like. Employees in the industrial sector with positions in marketing, sales, administration, finance, consulting, or customer support are also knowledge workers. They all have two things in common:

1. They reason on the basis of knowledge acquired mainly through their initial training, their experience, and the best practices of their companies. To put it another way, they apply their business rules to the specific context of their customers, whether they are external clients or internal colleagues. The requests may be more or less similar, but each person's situation is unique, and a knowledge worker takes each person's individual situation into account when offering advice or guidance.
2. They use language to communicate with their customers. Among this population, conversing is the day's

primary activity, accounting for far more time than is spent sleeping. Indeed, a study conducted by an American university states that knowledge workers spend between 70 and 80 percent of their waking time[4] (at least two-thirds of the day) using language to communicate. It is also important to note that reasoning and the use of language are so interconnected that it is difficult to separate them from each other. When a knowledge worker speaks or writes, they are in fact expressing their reasoning in natural language.

Finally, some knowledge workers occupy a dual position. A dentist is a knowledge worker when communicating with their client and making a diagnosis. Each knowledge worker applies their personal preferences and feelings when analyzing a situation or even when suggesting a solution. A dentist is also a craftsperson in the noble sense of the word when they use a drill to repair a cavity.

The potential for productivity gains from using AI to automate the work of knowledge workers is tremendous.

---

4 *Dick Lee and Delmar Hatesohl, "Listening: Our Most Used Communication Skill," University of Missouri, 1993, https://extension2.missouri.edu/cm150.*

The New Constraints of Twenty-First-Century Companies

As mentioned earlier, recent statistics show a drop in the productivity of knowledge workers. According to the human resources managers we interviewed, knowledge workers are frustrated with work they deem unnecessary and feel constantly overwhelmed. They believe that despite all their efforts, they are unable to provide services that fully meet their customers' expectations. According to our conversations,[5] four fundamental conditions are responsible for this constant feeling of lagging behind, which can be summarized as follows:

1. Data overload: There is so much customer information available that employees are just as lost as when there was no information at all.
2. Product overload: Companies are developing an increasing number of products or services to meet the needs of each customer segment and to differentiate themselves from the competition. Field teams, whether commercial or technical, are no longer able to retain the knowledge needed to adequately market an overly stocked portfolio or to properly guide customers through a technical support call.
3. Changes in regulation: The increase of best practices in each business sector, as well as increases in legislation, make providing products and services more complex. If a company does not abide by them, customers

5 *We contacted and surveyed an average of fifty decision makers per week over a twelve-month period.*

will not hesitate to complain publicly on social networks. Thus, any error can generate financial and image-related consequences.

4. The GAFA benchmark: Customers are accustomed to interacting with Google, Amazon, Facebook, and Apple (GAFA) in a digital environment where immediacy is the rule and customers demand that fast responses be available across all channels at any time of the day.

Let's look at each condition to explain the root causes of these new constraints.

The Four Conditions Knowledge Workers Face in the Twenty First Century

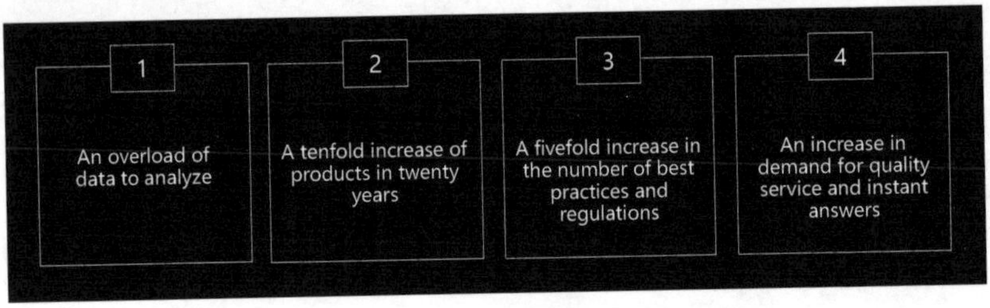

Too Much Information Kills Information

Knowledge workers have access to so much information that it is difficult to analyze it and use it effectively. Indeed, the historical decline in the cost of storage has enabled companies to collect an incredible amount of information on customers, prospects, products, the state of the company, and the market. But this approach to information technology (IT) actually became a victim of its own success. Companies collected as much data as possible before legislation like Europe's General Data Protection Regulation (GDPR) went into effect. Big data promoters' sales pitch was simple: If your employees don't have information, they are blind. So the more information they have, the more informed (and therefore correct) their decisions will be.

Unfortunately, this reasoning is flawed. American psychologist George A. Miller observed after many experiments that a human being could retain only seven points of information in their short-term memory. In other words, the human brain is easily overwhelmed by multiple pieces of information. This can delay or adversely affect decision-making.

Of course, when a knowledge worker uses their professional memory (different from their short-term memory because it is acquired and retained over the long term), they are able to reason with a larger amount of data. It has been said that in aeronautics, for example, aircraft pilots are able to consider up to thirty parameters for a landing. This is consistent with what we see in real life. For example, a few years ago, we hired an employee who happened to be a bridge champion. While playing with him, outside the context of work, we observed that at the end of each deal, he could recite from memory the order and content of each fold of four cards. His professional memory perfectly trained in bridge allowed him to memorize fifty-two cards and therefore to reason with up to fifty points or so of information before choosing the best card to play next. While this type of professional memory is uncommon, a human capacity to train one's brain to use a larger amount of information is possible.

Let's say that thirty points is likely to be the maximum data set number our brain can process in our professional memory. How many different data points does your customer relationship management (CRM) contain for each customer—one hundred, two hundred, or more? With ten customers a day and hundreds of data points for each one of them, how can a sales or marketing person reason and make the best decisions? In this context, the question is whether collecting so much information is really useful in the end. With such a large volume of data, doesn't it become harder to find the most useful information? Ultimately, excessive data collection to better inform knowledge workers makes them more confused and may actually be counterproductive.

Yet in an ideal world, an efficient knowledge worker would be able to take advantage of this wealth of available information, analyze it, extract what is most important, make better decisions, and better serve their customers. This knowledge worker does not exist. Or, rather, they do not exist without the help of AI. The more data we collect, the greater the need for AI to interpret and synthesize it. This is the first economic reason that makes collaborative AI increasingly essential.

A Growing Number of Products and Services You Need to Know About

Another condition that knowledge workers are facing today is the increased number of products or services their company markets. The challenge becomes not only knowing the characteristics of these products and services but also how to position them for a prospect (which customer profile is the best match?), how to sell them without giving misleading advice, how to install them correctly for customers, and how to maintain them. A company's goal is laudable but challenging: to gain market share by opening up new market segments thanks to differentiated products with high added value that generate growth and better margins.

In business, the strategy of selling a wide variety of specialty products to a small pool of customers is a basic trend that started in the digital world. Chris Anderson, the former editor-in-chief of *WIRED* magazine, described it very well in his 2004 article "The Long Tail."[6] For example, a book that tops the best-seller list will be available in all bookstores, but a book that focuses on a specific field and costs much more than a paperback will be available only in specialized bookstores or online. This strategy of producing more sophisticated and better-targeted products to gain markets and increase margins is attractive on paper. However, the logistics needed to set up the sale of, and support for, more complex products (such as financial products, cars, or custom kitchens) are much more intricate than those associated with scaling up simple products like paperbacks.

We can clearly observe this in the retail market of the banking sector. At the end of the 1990s, a financial adviser would market a dozen financial products: checking accounts, savings accounts, loans, retirement plans, and so on. In most countries today, to do their job, an adviser has to be familiar with more than one hundred financial products, at least in theory. The consequence is simple. Because advisers' brains have not

6 *Chris Anderson, "Th e Long Tail," Wired, October 1, 2004, http://www.wired.com/2004/10/tail.*

grown tenfold, they have not processed the majority of the new products offered, even if they do know their names and a few of their features. As a result, they do not sell the products, including those with high margins, that are best suited to the customer but rely instead on the products they know well—namely, the most basic products they think sell the best. These products generate little value for customers and smaller margins for the organization due to their availability among competitors, including low-cost online platforms. Companies are aware of this problem and are trying to solve it with a specialized workforce, thereby increasing the complexity of their internal organization. As a consequence, an adviser will go back and forth with centralized experts who they contact remotely and who are supposed to help them better target their market and explain which financial products best match a customer's needs. Although this overabundance of products and services has proved to be counterproductive, it seems impossible to step back now due to the great risk of falling into the low-cost company trap, where price is all that matters and everything else goes by the wayside. As we will see later in this chapter, collaborative AI not only solves this headache but also encourages a profusion of offers. This increase in products and services forces companies to equip themselves with new AI approach to better assist knowledge workers so that the company can pursue a premium model, where the personalized customer support and expert service are outstanding.

Best Practices and Compliance

The third upheaval our companies and their employees are facing is tied to their sector of operation's business rules and the compliance mechanisms implemented through those rules, standards, standardizations, and certifications. Here are some examples of new rules that affect businesses:

• Regulations: Every market is facing new and complex regulations like the Dodd–Frank Wall Street Reform and Consumer Protection Act in the United States following the banking crisis, the CCPA Act in California or GDPR in Europe.

• Certifications: To reassure patients, companies work hard to receive HIPAA certification, which allows the storage of personal health data.

• Standards: Request for proposal procedures are often imposed by companies and governments to enable purchasing and potential suppliers to transmit information to one another.

• Standardizations: Within large companies, standardizations ensure that all subsidiaries apply the same best practices and offer a consistent level of service to their customers.

Initiatives that increase compliance and automation of processes are taken with good intentions and, on paper, do improve transparency and market performance. However, the increase in obligations results in additional new constraints at each stage of a company's value chain, be it the sale of a product, delivery, customer support, marketing, or, more generally, initiative and innovation. Increased rules add to the complexity of running a business and reduce the productivity of knowledge workers.

An Increasingly Demanding Customer Service

The latest constraint observed by many companies is that of customer demands. Indeed, as a result of the emergence of digital-first companies, such as GAFA, customers now want access to immediate service.

The following scenario is representative of the reality described by the executives we interviewed:

- Before calling a supplier and asking for advice, the customer goes online to gather information.
- When they contact the company to request a product or service, they expect to speak to a knowledgeable person immediately because they have already researched the matter and even believe they know everything there is to know about the subject.
- Customers are more and more demanding and expect a near instant answer without realizing that in many companies, many service processes remain traditional ones. A business consultancy proposal or a personalized offer requires human intervention, especially when a discussion is necessary to justify the technical choices and the cost.

As AI can help solve these problems, it becomes both essential and urgent.

The Effect of Conventional Information Technology on Knowledge Workers

Knowledge workers spend a large part of their day working on computers, and an increasing share of their activity is digitized. However, this digitization has not resulted in productivity gains similar to those brought on by computers, especially in industrial production companies. It is critical to understand the effect of conventional IT on the work of knowledge workers to identify AI's potential and how it can address slumping productivity. For this, one must analyze the three tasks that knowledge workers perform in a day:

1. They collect information about the work to be done, either by accessing computer data or by interacting with their customers (internal or external) to get more details regarding their needs.
2. They process the information collected based on the rules they learned during training, their experience, their cultural background, and according to the best practices of the company where they work.
3. They express their conclusions in spoken or written language in a summary of the situation, a diagnosis, and a reasoned recommendation. They might also guide a customer through a business process.

Three Tasks Knowledge Workers Perform Daily

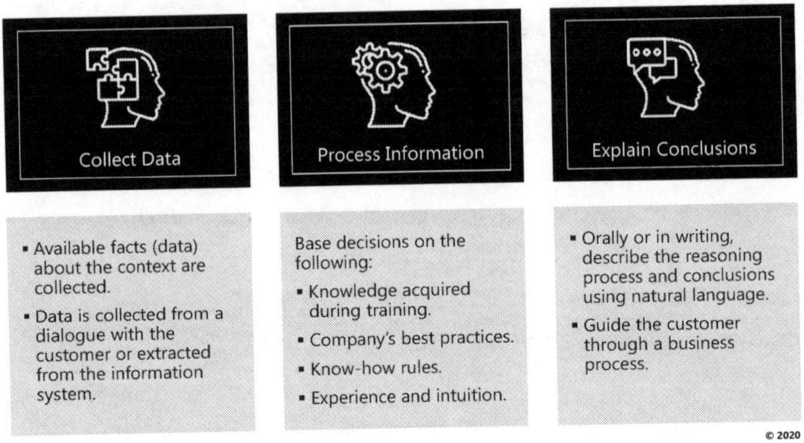

These three steps apply regardless of the knowledge worker's profession: adviser, marketer, salesperson, manager, doctor, lawyer, architect, and so on.

Service activities, whether carried out within service companies or within the executive management, marketing, sales, or support departments of industrial companies, have evolved over the past decades with the deployment of computer software intended to help knowledge workers become more productive. According to a 2017 Orbis Research study, these general-purpose application software packages mostly consist of the following—if we classify them by the revenue they generate:

- CRM: Software in which all customer relationship information is available in one place.
- Enterprise resource planning (ERP): Software in which various business departments (finance, production, sales, and marketing) can better share information thanks to this single centralized data model.

• Business intelligence (BI): Software that allows executives to visualize the company's aggregated data in real time or near real time to understand what's happening and to identify leads to make progress toward and achieve business goals.

We will further discuss these software packages as examples that illustrate what conventional IT has been concentrating on these past fifty years—the tasks where it excels: data collection, storage, calculation, and communication between computers.

In the service sector, of the knowledge worker's three tasks, only their access to company and customer information has increased in productivity thanks to conventional IT. Whether they use a CRM, ERP, or BI tool, knowledge workers spend less time searching for internal documents and customer information today than they did twenty years ago, provided the search query is simple enough and they know what they are looking for. They also have access to external information databases with search engines, but their effectiveness is called into question by search engine optimization (SEO) and search engine advertising (SEA), business strategies to climb up Google's lists, therefore influencing the order of search results. There is also a lack of any dialogue engine to refine searches, or, to put it another way, the systems assume that the knowledge worker knows what they are looking for and don't allow for questions to help them dig deeper and find what they are truly looking for. On the other hand, for tasks that require applying a reasoning on facts and expressing their conclusions in natural language, the knowledge worker remains on their own, without any tools to help them. Yet it is their core business.

Here's an example to illustrate our point: A salesperson prepares a telephone appointment with a customer to take stock of their business relationship and to possibly sell additional services. A CRM would certainly help the salesperson find the history of exchanges between this customer and the company as long as it has been regularly updated (but lack of use of CRMs in business is a major problem and a dirty little secret that many would not admit publicly). The salesperson would easily be able to see the latest price offer, the support calls the customer may have placed, and any brochures that were sent to the customer. Some CRMs may even trigger suggestions of actions to take based on the information collected. These suggestions may include products for sale or even generate prefilled contracts. But this time-saver would not allow our salesperson to guarantee the customer the right advice or support. To do that, the salesperson must do the following:

• Collect the customer's information and interact with the customer to understand their context and to be able to adapt the offer to fit the situation. If, for instance, the customer has just acquired another company, it may be time to offer other services adapted to their new challenges.

• Always rely on best practices and their own experience to decide how they will conduct the meeting.

• Explain the conclusions of their reasoning and why the suggested product or service will perfectly meet the needs of the customer. The salesperson must then specify what steps to take to order the service. The only help available to them is generic and static rules (the knowledge they learned in their training, the best practices of the company, and their experience). It is up to the salesperson to adapt them to the context of the customer. Thus, the quality of the individualized expertise they deliver is tied to their own competence. Or, to put it another way, the quality of the service the customer gets depends on the quality of the salesperson assigned to them.

To summarize, conventional IT has helped increase productivity in industrial production because it has deeply influenced the core of the business: production of goods and logistics. For service activities, IT certainly makes information easier to store, easier to search (provided that the request is simple), and easier to transmit. But conventional software, or software that does not leverage AI, is confined to secondary tasks. The knowledge worker is on their own when applying their knowledge to a specific context and justifying their offer and reasoning in natural language..

This explains the heterogeneity within the same service company, as exemplified by differences in performance between salespeople on the same team who sell the same products or services and differences in the quality of answers among support technicians on the same call center platform.

As we will later discuss in the book, AI technologies such as machine learning and computer language management software will provide real answers to the limits just described.

The Need to Automate Individualized Human Expertise

As previously mentioned, customer demand is pressing for quality in services, and employers are complaining about the growing difficulty of recruiting qualified employees, with 60 percent saying it is taking more than twelve weeks to fill key roles.[7] Despite various governments' efforts to improve the training of their citizens, the lack of available qualified people in the labor market will remain an obstacle to economic development. Today, collaborative AI is the only solution to offer quality services on a large scale and at affordable prices. For the first time in history since the Industrial Revolution, technology will provide an answer to this challenge and even upend our approach to the automation of services. The internet has digitized information. AI will digitize the notion of individualized expertise, which can be defined as the application of knowledge to a particular context, such as a customer's question and unique situation. Until now, services were, by definition, human. Collaborative AI scales services that are individualized, reliable, and homogeneous in quality—and at an acceptable cost.

---

7 *Roy Maurer, "Training People for Jobs to Fill the Skills Gap," SHRM, September 7, 2017, http://www.shrm.org/resourcesandtools/hr-topics/talent-acquisition/pages/training-people-for-jobs-to-solve-the-nations-skills-gap.aspx.*

The Four Elements of the Collaborative AI Led Revolution in Services

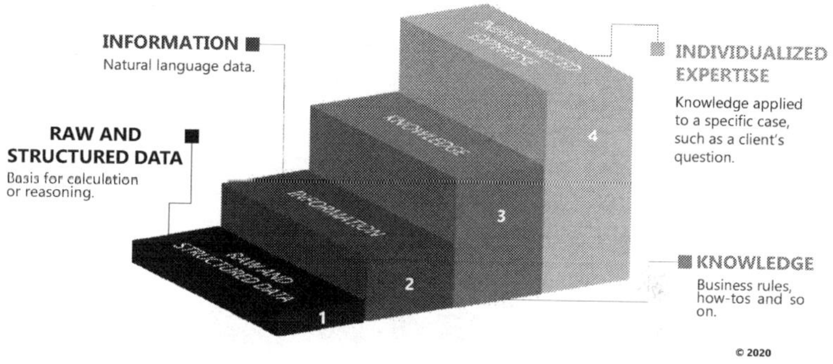

The cost of expertise will fall, just as that of information did gradually over a period of twenty or thirty years as it became digitalized. In the long term, the advice of a lawyer, a doctor, or any expert in the broad sense of the word will be worth only a few dollars. Only noble work, which will develop considerably, will remain the prerogative of human experts. Noble work is that which requires the intervention of human conscience, the taking into account of human relations, empathy, value judgment, creativity, or even of an uncommon task that has not yet been modeled. It requires thought and common sense. Up to 80 percent of knowledge workers' repetitive tasks, which most often do not require any thought, will be automated, with the same goal as that of robots employed in industry: to increase the quality and homogeneity of the answers and solutions developed on a large scale and at a lower cost. We will experience the transition from the digitalized information era, available to all, to the partial dematerialization of individualized expertise—and consequently, a significant reduction in the cost of advice, some of which may even become free. This "industrial revolution" of services that we call collaborative AI could bring us economic growth of the same magnitude as that enjoyed during the Renaissance. While such a rich period of history was characterized economically by industrialization and the democratization of knowledge thanks to Gutenberg's printing press, AI allows the democratization not of knowledge but of expertise—that is to say, individualized advice in the broad sense of the term, provided by knowledge workers at a high hourly cost. Service companies that fail to automate expertise for their customers will disappear. In chapter 5, we will discuss why collaborative AI increases employment or more precisely the need of knowledge workers. On the other hand, there is no doubt that the nature of their day-to-day activities will change fundamentally, but these changes will be positive.

Service tasks performed by knowledge workers are becoming increasingly important in business, but conventional IT tools have not been able to help them effectively in their core activity. IT has mainly brought value to the peripheral tasks of service activities. In addition, the overabundance of information, the growing number of products and services to market and maintain, the increased number of business and compliance rules, and the demands of customers make service tasks increasingly complicated to manage. The search for solutions becomes increasingly urgent. Thus, beyond technological progress, the AI revolution is driven by these compelling economic reasons. It will be mainly geared toward service activities, where productivity and employee comfort gains stand to be the greatest. This is why the future of AI for the next decades to come is collaborative AI.

Based on this analysis, this new approach will drive three main positive disruptions for knowledge workers:

1. The automation of some repetitive tasks that require little creative thought, thus slowly relieving overwhelmed employees.
2. Cobots, or collaborative robots, in the form of AI-based software that augment the intelligence of knowledge workers without replacing them. Work becomes a synergy between knowledge worker and machine.
3. Augmented marketing that combines one-on-one sales with the limitless ability to create customized products and services. Marketing becomes a more effective communication channel between a company's creativity and production capabilities and its sales department. Collaborative AI opens the way for marketing that is no longer based on information but on expertise as a vector for development.

Based on our past experience deploying many collaborative AI projects, we will expand these use cases in the next chapters. For these innovative solutions to realize their synergy potential and drive—a new industrial revolution—a strong value proposition must emerge. We believe we are on the cusp of a paradigm shift where AI will move from being cool to being crucial and collaborative.

2.

Automation of Repetitive Tasks in the Service Sector

As machines become more and more efficient and perfect, so it will become clear that imperfection is the greatness of man.

Ernst Fischer, Austrian writer

Now that we have defined collaborative artificial intelligence, let's cover the first use case, the one most easily imagined: the automation of repetitive tasks. The more AI advances, the more human work it can take on. This approach may sound alarming, but it will probably prove to be an exceptional factor of both economic growth and quality-of-life improvement for employees. Similarly, though reviled in its day, the invention of the printing press largely contributed to the advent of the Renaissance, a period of strong economic growth in Europe that lasted between the end of the fifteenth century and the beginning of the seventeenth century. This chapter further develops how AI allows the automation of repetitive tasks, also named RPA[8], with examples based on our experience that provide concrete ideas that you can implement in your company.

We all know what an industrial robot can do in a factory, which is to repeat the same movements with speed and precision. Today, many industrial manufacturers' development plans rely on robotization to produce custom-made goods almost at the same price as their mass-producing competitors. Schmidt Kitchens[9] , whose marketing slogan was "Custom-Made Is No Longer a Luxury," was among the first to establish the benefits

---

8 *RPA means robot processing automation and implies the use of software with, most of the time, AI algorithms to automate repetitive tasks that previously required humans to perform.*

9 *https://www.groupe.schmidt/en/home-en/*

of automation for both company success and employee well-being. Today, however, the application of AI to task automation still faces cultural challenges tied to some negative perceptions and the difficulty nonexperts have in understanding its practical uses in the service sector.

First of all, despite technological progress, it is hard to imagine that a software program could automate service tasks, as it requires reasoning, communicating in natural language, and producing individualized results to match each customer's context. Yet this use of AI is already occurring in the most innovative companies. We will explain later why this approach is an integral part of collaborative AI.

The second cultural challenge concerns the other widely held belief that automating tasks threatens employment. The best way to address this challenge is to look at previous innovations and how those changes affected business and society. Although the following examples are not part of modern AI, the numbers imply, in hindsight, that task automation is actually more likely to create jobs:

• Germany, the European leader in industrial robotics with nearly thirty industrial robots per thousand employees, is enjoying its best period of full employment since the 1990 German reunification.[10]

• Since the 1990s, accountants and auditors have been using bookkeeping and management software that automates the core of their work with tremendous efficiency. Yet software

---

10 *"How Reunification Is Going—How Far a Once-Divided Germany Has Grown Together Again," Berlin Institute, July 2015, http://www.berlin-institut.org/fileadmin/user_upload/So_geht_Einheit/BI_SoGehtEinheit_final_online.pdf.*

did not come close to replacing accountants. From 1993 to 2008, in the middle of an accounting-management software sales boom, the demand for accountants in the United States continued to outpace other sectors.[11] In fact, today the Bureau of Labor Statistics believes that the demand for accountants will continue to grow at 10 percent more than average despite all the advances and the adoption of technology.[12] Computer science has changed the nature of accountants' work so that they now spend less time on data entry and more time on financial forecasting analysis.

- In the automobile industry, often named one of the most automated sectors, employment increased by 35 percent in the United States from 2009 to 2019.[13]

In all these examples, it is fair to say that the actual work being done by employees changed and evolved, but it is clear that automation had not been a net negative in some of the most highly automated sectors. Given that AI will automate in a similar although more advanced fashion, it is safe to assume that the results of AI on employment figures will be minimal and might even spur growth in certain areas. Finally, practical examples

---

11 *Arlene Dohm and Lynn Shniper, "Occupational Employment Projections to 2016," Monthly Labor Review, November 2007, http://www.bls.gov/opub/mlr/2007/11/art5full.pdf.*

12 *"Accountants and Auditors," Occupational Outlook Handbook, US Bureau of Labor Statistics, last modified September 4, 2019, http:// www.bls.gov/ooh/business-and-financial/accountants-and-auditors.htm.*

13 *"All Employees, Thousands, Motor Vehicles and Parts, Seasonally Adjusted," US Bureau of Labor Statistics, December 18, 2019, https://data.bls.gov/timeseries/CES3133600101?amp%3bdata_tool=XGtable&output_view=data&include_graphs=true.*

later in the book based on our experience will show that AI does not stand on its own but rather amid an ecosystem of technologies. Indeed, most AI-based applications rely on other different technologies, thereby offering expanded possibilities.

Why Is It Necessary to Automate?

Automation is necessary mainly on two levels. First, it can support tasks that require little creativity, common sense or empathy. Such tasks can be seen as a waste of time by the company's employees and can become a source of demotivation when they are too frequent, especially among knowledge workers. In the end, performing these tasks runs up high costs for the company, when wasted time and consequent lack of motivation are taken into account. The banking sector provides a powerful example here. When you talk to management in this sector, they say that hiring and keeping good talent is one of their biggest challenges because they face high staff turnover.[14] They recruit from the best universities, yet many of these young people are simply bored by the repetitive tasks they are being asked to do on a daily basis.

Second, automation can relieve employees of tasks deemed too complex, those for which the human brain is not best suited, such as the analysis of large volumes of data. This

14 *Tim Ufer, "The Millennial Turnover Problem in the Financial Services Industry," Hppy, accessed October 11, 2019, https://gethppy.com/employee-turnover/the-millennial-turnover-problem-in-the-financial-services-industry. Figures vary, with some putting the turnover rate as a high as 18 percent. Many argue that this is driven by employees who feel that they aren't able to make a difference.*

becomes a great opportunity for companies to improve both working conditions and productivity. It also grants knowledge workers the freedom to focus on value-added tasks, such as noble work that robots are not able to do—work that requires common sense, creativity, and empathy, among other qualities. Automation is therefore a motivating element. But does that mean all tasks, from the simplest to the most complex, should be automated? What are the keys to strategically selecting which tasks to optimize in service activities?

What Processes Should Be Automated?

The first factor in determining whether a task should be automated is its suitability for outsourcing. Indeed, subcontracting to an external service provider or to a robot is a similar process. It is necessary to precisely model the task to be automated and to train involved parties to absorb this know-how or to configure the system. It should be noted that delegating work to AI does not present any risk of intellectual property loss for the company, whereas passing on know-how to a third party may risk turning the partner into a competitor. In any case, if a task that does not require human qualities such as creativity, common sense, or empathy to be outsourced, it is ready to be automated.

The second factor is the volume of production coupled with the repetitiveness of the task. The more repetitive a task, the more it should be automated. Conversely, such a process is not industrialized just to produce a few units unless the complexity of the task or the quality of the production requires it. This approach, tried and tested in industrial production, is also valid for the service sector.

Although the ability of a task to be outsourced and the end volume of production remain the most critical elements when considering automation, there is in fact another important factor to address—a much more strategic one. The massive adoption of a service by consumers and businesses is often linked to a drop in its price, as was the case with mobile phones and air travel. Automation of a service task, which drastically reduces its production costs, makes it available to a much larger number of customers. This is an important facet of collaborative AI: the price of the service is mostly set according to the added value perceived by the customer, not by its production cost. Lowering the cost of a service, thanks to AI-led automation, can represent a real competitive advantage with three practical implications:

1. Sales could be increased by a factor of fifty, one hundred, or more thanks to the opening up of new markets. It is no longer the actual volume of production that must be taken into account to justify the automation process. Rather, it is the potential market volume when the cost of the service becomes significantly lower and attracts many new customers who would not have purchased it had the price remained higher.

2. Because the service process is automated, there are no longer any constraints to producing a quality service in high volume.

3. Complete automation of a task reduces the overall production cost to that of the initial setup investment for

> the automated service, as the automation incurs an almost insignificant ongoing cost of production. This is especially true of intellectual services, which have no inventory management restrictions because the basic product is gray matter (knowledge). The gross margin and the sales generated by this automated service are then one and the same. The business becomes very profitable.

In short, thanks to the smart adoption of collaborative AI, you can do more and do it better and faster, allowing you to offer your service to more people than ever before. In this context, automation does not so much eliminate jobs as it creates new services. This is the first giant leap that this AI approach will bring to the economies of countries whose GDP is essentially based on services. We could be witnessing the largest gains in productivity in the service sector since the Industrial Revolution.

As in industrial production, automating a service task requires clearly defined delivery processes. Each service or consulting task to be outsourced must be broken down into three parts, and the project manager must consider the following questions to determine how to automate it:

- Reasoning: Am I able to describe the business logic and supporting data of the task to automate? Am I automating a task that requires an exact and precise outcome (one that is determinist and controllable) or one that accepts an approximate statistical result?
- Digitized online dialogue or voice assistant: Regarding the new service, what level of understanding of user questions

is critical for my project? Can I opt for predefined questions or even close-ended questions?

• Expression of the reasoning's conclusions in natural language: Where language treatment is concerned, the mistake would be to focus only on natural language understanding (NLU), as with such tools as Siri or Dragon Mobile Assistant. How should the conclusions be delivered? In the form of a spreadsheet with charts or rather with a situation summary, diagnosis, or reasoned recommendations?

The answers to these questions will also determine the type of technology and even the tools to use for your AI project.

Finally, automation of a task should be progressive. The correct approach is probably not to automate everything at once but to do so incrementally, as we will discuss at the end of this chapter.

The Technical Choices Related to Task Automation

Task automation by AI requires tackling some technical issues. Although chapter 6 is dedicated to these topics, it is important to mention the two basic types of modern technical approaches to defining and producing the business rules or algorithms that govern a reasoning process.

The first pillar of AI is having a system that is able to reason automatically and the most publicized is machine learning. Simply put, ML replaces part of the work of computer scientists, who used to spend months or even years developing reasoning algorithms that are now, in part, automatically generated by AI in just a few days or weeks.

The most commonly used ML software technology is referred to as neural networks. They are based on a statistical method, on available data averages that AI uses to generate algorithms. Neural networks are a series of data processing nodes designed to mimic the communication structure of the human brain. It's a common myth that machine learning requires no development time and that it is a sort of magic plug-and-play tool. The truth is that machine learning, like all technology, requires development time to prepare the data being mined and then computing time for the system to set the objective and analyze the data test cases. While new technologies such as automated machine learning offer promise, the challenge is the sheer volume of data that machine learning requires. Because it is based on probability, the more data or test cases, the more accurate the output will be. The requirement for large amounts of data with strong data governance in place explains why Google, Facebook, and Amazon are the leaders in the ML space. They have the cloud-computing infrastructure, large amounts of data, and qualified people to implement ML projects.

This stands in contrast to the second technical approach: deterministic reasoning processes that always react the same way to an event. These expert systems, most often relying on inference engines, are certainly less powerful than neural networks because handwritten rules are their reasoning logic. On the other hand, they do guarantee 100 percent accurate results if the rules are correct—a bit like Microsoft Excel when the calculation formulas are correctly defined. In many professions, rigor, legal risk, and a quality approach prohibit approximation. What would you say if the IRS announced that this year's tax calculation was based on statistics and therefore the amount you owe is roughly 80 percent correct? Every taxpayer wants to understand how their tax is calculated and make sure that calculation is accurate. Only certain tasks, such as trend analysis or, to some extent in the service sector, commercial targeting, can be automated with an ML statistically based technology. The levels of detail and accuracy of AI-based results often exceed what people can achieve manually in an equivalent period of time. Most service tasks to be automated require a deterministic method with perfectly accurate and traceable reasoning. Therefore, the automation of many business processes relies on inference engines (expert systems) that already provide significant advances over traditional programming. You will be able to select the appropriate method, approach, and technology after analyzing your automation needs.

It should be noted that the AI available on the market today is known as weak AI. In fact, we find that once we understand how AI works (whether machine learning driven or expert system driven), it loses its magic and people don't believe it's real AI. We expect AI magic to be inexplicable. Some have called this the AI effect.[15] Many of us think of true AI as being able to carry out any task a human can. This would require multidisciplinary

---

15 *This is often attributed to Pamela McCorduck, Machines Who Think: A Personal Inquiry into the History and Prospects of Artificial Intelligence, 2nd ed. (Boca Raton, FL: CRC Press, 2004).*

AI, or artificial general intelligence (AGI) that does not exist yet. DeepMind's[16] AlphaZero platform remains a specialist system: It requires an independent learning phase to generate distinct algorithms to play the games of Go, chess, and shogi. And its training in one game field does not help it win in another. Despite these current limitations, most AI experts foresee the availability of AGI by the end of this century. But who knows? Perhaps by then the definition of *real AI* will have progressed further, and we will think of this generalist AI simply as computing.

Meanwhile, the inability of weak AI to adapt to different situations instantly, to be truly creative (the management of unexpected situations, for example), and to have common sense or empathy fundamentally limits automation and therefore the possibility of AI replacing employees. Indeed, these qualities are essential to understanding customers, and their needs and feelings, especially in the service sector, which aims to provide answers adapted to their requests.

Once you have a system that is able to reason (no matter whether it uses ML or an expert system), you need to focus on the best way to share the results of that reasoning process with human beings.

The second pillar of AI is the use of language to communicate. In fact, the importance of language to AI goes all the way back to one of the fathers of AI, Alan Turing and his famous Turing test, which foresaw machines dialoguing seamlessly with human beings. For our purposes, to automate a service task, the computer must understand, ask intelligent

16 *DeepMind is a British company dedicated to AI that was acquired by Alphabet Inc. (Google's parent company) in 2014.*

questions, and generate answers in spoken or written language in the specific language of its contact person.

To fully understand the challenge of language processing by computers and to make the right automation choice from a business point of view, we must examine the types of information that knowledge workers manage and use to successfully do their jobs. A human is able to understand or memorize only five categories of information (we're excluding the emotional component): raw data, structured data, language data, knowledge, and expertise. As we said before, AGI doesn't exist yet, so each of these categories corresponds with an area of computer science research. From the beginning of any automation project, it is important to determine the kind of text you want to produce—for instance, answers—and the type of available data.

This brings us to detail the five elements encountered during the automation of a service task. They can be upstream (to feed AI) or downstream (to be produced by AI) from an automation process:

1. Raw data is meaningless data to a computer. When you receive an email, a PowerPoint presentation, or a Word file, current software does not understand the meaning of the messages contained in these documents. At best, it identifies a few key words and guesses the content based on statistics. This is raw data. Photos are also raw data, although AI can usually identify the content, and considerable progress continues to be made in this area. To be fully exploited by computers, data must be structured.

2. Structured data is understandable by a computer because it is labeled. Let's take the example of the Excel spreadsheet. Each number is at the intersection of a column and a line whose meaning is clearly defined: it is a price, a revenue, a weight, a telephone number, a customer account identifier, and so on. The most critical data in a management system must be structured.

3. Natural language data, often called information, can be in English, Spanish, French, or any other language or dialect provided that some human beings understand it. This language is used for communication between people. Google, for instance, is a natural language information search engine. You type in your question with words, and the engine returns results that are essentially matches to natural language documents (with extensions, you also get images and graphics).

4. Knowledge is another element to take into account when automating a task. Knowledge can be defined simply as "how to." Scanning all the books in the world's libraries has been one of Google's most important (and discreet) areas of development for many years. Why? The creators of the California search engine understood that the research market would evolve from information to knowledge. By working on software that can assign correct meaning to the content of each book (NLU), Google grants itself the unique opportunity of offering a service in the future that specifically searches and compares knowledge. The example of a cooking recipe illustrates

the difference between information and knowledge: the list of ingredients is information in natural language, but the written recipe itself is knowledge. The author explains how to mix and cook the ingredients and in what order.

In a professional context, business rules govern the how-to and are therefore generic: how to write an invoice, how to change a defective spare part, or how to calculate a production cost. To answer how-to questions requires knowledge, which is a generalist notion therefore not linked to any specific context. For instance, it is common for us to read a document of ten pages or so and then realize that only two paragraphs present a real interest for our context, and yet they still don't address our specific issue. Or that after reading the document, we have even more questions than before because our context is different from the one mentioned in the document. Building useful knowledge traditionally requires human intelligence for a contextual interpretation. It should be noted that although books have been the essential source of knowledge for more than five centuries thanks to Gutenberg's industrialization of printing, today's how-to videos most often also belong to the world of knowledge. For the automation of a task, business rules that represent the reasoning logic of a business process are an integral part of knowledge.

5. Individualized expertise rounds off this list because customers are fond of it, and before the latest generation of AI software reached the market, no computer program had been able to automate its production. Individualized

expertise is a thought process that applies generic how-to rules learned from training, best practices, and experience to the specific and possibly unique context of a situation. In other words, it is the application of knowledge to a particular case, such as a question from an internal or external client. Individualized expertise is what any consulting entity produces, whether it's a law firm, a hospital, an accounting firm, an architect, a call center, a mediator, or even a garage mechanic (doing a breakdown diagnosis).

Let's use a lawyer as an example. In the traditional model, the lawyer will first listen to a client describe the context of their problem. The lawyer will ask specific questions to collect the data points needed to make a correct recommendation. They will then present their reasoning as an analysis of the situation from a legal point of view and propose a well-argued solution based on knowledge and experience. It may materialize, for example, as a letter to be sent to the opposite party. The added value the lawyer brings is what we call individualized expertise. Until the advent of AI, only human beings could go through this process. With today's available AI, producing individualized expertise can be automated, rendering its cost independent from the volume of requests. As soon as the system works for a targeted use, the only cost is that of the electricity used to run the computer. Automating the production of individualized expertise will revolutionize the service sector's business model without replacing workers by the machine, whatever their level of expertise as described later.

For each project, you must determine which elements are available to feed AI (raw and/or structured data, natural language information) and what type(s) of answers (knowledge or individualized expertise) you want to receive from AI. Let's look at some examples of applications, based on our field experience, that automate tasks in the service sector. You will see why the production of individualized and digitized expertise is a revolution of the same magnitude as the industrialization of knowledge from Gutenberg's printing press. In the following scenarios, there are additional sections regarding the type of data or elements that were used or produced. Of course, the configuration times are for illustration purposes only. The goal here is mainly to suggest concrete application ideas for your company or department.

As a reminder, here is a small lexicon of technical terms—also included in this book's glossary—with simplified explanations that will figure in the following use case scenarios:

• Machine learning (ML) software: This software analyzes data prepared by computer scientists and generates its own reasoning algorithms from predefined goals. It requires significant volumes of data to be relevant.

• Neural networks: Computing algorithms that are mostly used to power ML systems. Neural networks learn to perform tasks by considering examples. The method and structure of the processing loosely resembles the communication process of neurons in our biological brain.

• Expert systems: Any software that develops reasoning algorithms based on rules manually written by a business expert, most often without having to use any type of static "if . . . then . . . if not" decision tree. A decision tree is a treelike graph in which each node represents a test on a criterion. For example, if it rains, I'll take an umbrella. If not, I'll leave it at home. The notion of an expert system is often related to that of first-generation artificial intelligence. There is no self-learning, but the system is rigorously accurate (deterministic) and widely deployed around the world. Its reliability for modest-size applications (up to a few hundred rules) and its ease of use are indisputable and therefore may be a wise choice for SMEs.

• Natural language understanding (NLU): Any software that recognizes text or voice and understands their meaning to a certain extent.

• Natural language generation (NLG): Any software aimed at generating intelligent text from data analysis.

• Minimum viable (and virtuous) product (MVP): In our context, an MVP is a new application with enough features to satisfy initial users in order to obtain feedback.

• Robot processing automation (RPA): Where software is used to automate repetitive tasks, using AI most of the time.

• Virtual reality (VR): An artificial simulation of a real-life environment or situation where the user feels like they are experiencing a new reality.

• Augmented reality (AR): A technology that adds computer-generated enhancements atop an existing real-life environment or situation in order to augment it with new features.

Scenario 1: Free Online Diagnosis

Your company makes hair care products. The success of these products lies in their unique quality composition and a wide product segmentation that meets the specific needs of each type of hair. You had chosen to rely on the expertise of a network of hair stylists and resellers. This allowed you to offer some consulting as well, so your customers could be directed to the right product for their hair type and informed of its proper use. However, this model is reaching its limits because hair stylists tend to be conservative in their buying habits. You also don't really know your customer because the business model is really B2B to C, meaning the hair stylists know the customer, not you. In order to meet your growth objectives, you want to take the leap to online sales.

Description of the automation solution: You can set up a free diagnostic solution on your website. The dynamic questionnaire identifies the type of hair, the lifestyle habits, the treatments currently used, the potential minor hair issues, and the objective sought by applying the treatment. At the end of the two-minute questionnaire, the user sees on the web page a complete hair diagnosis, a list of two to three recommended treatment products (shampoo, conditioner, oil, serum, etc.), and advice in terms of use (method and time of application) according to their specific hair type.

Gains obtained:

- You collect a lot of data on your prospective customers.
- You sell the products that meet the prospective customers' needs, not those that a hair stylist likes and has been recommending for the past ten years without giving your new innovative products a chance.
- Your new customers are likely to get good results because the advice you give is well adapted to their needs.
- You cultivate your customers' loyalty as they become satisfied with your products. Thanks to word of mouth, even hair stylists will hear about them because their customers will surely ask for your new products.
- You could set up a new method of subscription marketing by monitoring the progress noted by each customer through a monthly email questionnaire and fine-tuning the treatment you send out each month.
- You build a high-end business marketing image that focuses on relevant and effective individualized recommendations.

AI technologies used: Expert system, ML, and NLG to write the recommendations.

Configuration or setup time for an MVP:[17] Forty to fifty human days. We refer to an eight-hour workday in this book.

Types of data or elements used and produced: At the input, the questionnaire data is structured; at the output from AI, the

---

17 *A minimum viable (and virtuous) product (MVP) is a draft of an application. An MVP not only proves that it brings return on investment to the company but also that it provides a solution to a real business issue.*

diagnosis provided is individualized expertise in the form of text displayed on a web page.

Scenario 2: Your Customers Update Your CRM

Your company is a car rental corporation, leasing company cars to business customers. You have deployed CRM software, but almost no one puts data into it. Your employees perceive it as keeping tabs on them and therefore avoid contributing any customer information whenever possible. The actual goal of the CRM was to help them close more business, but with no data in the system, it is not delivering value for you. In short, the return on investment (ROI) from the implementation of this solution is not good, especially because the CRM information, when it does appear in the database, is of poor quality.

Description of the automation solution: Rather than relying on your employees to feed the CRM, encourage your customers to do this by offering them a reward, such as in exchange for answering an individualized questionnaire, they will receive free expert advice. You may suggest to your customers that they will receive a short monthly report (one page maximum) that advises them, in an individualized manner, on how to manage the products or services you offer, as if a consultant were to meet them for one hour every month to take stock of their situation. To further convince them, you can send them an email with a sample report that proves the value offered. The contents of this monthly report could show, for example, that a certain customer's employee is driving too much and may exceed the miles' allowance. To avoid paying a penalty at the end of the contract, the car could be rotated the following month with that of another person who drives less, and so on.

A maintenance or loyalty card gives access to a lot of interesting information that can be used as a basis for reasoning. You can also ask your customer for additional information—should they express their interest by clicking on a link in the email—that you don't have in your CRM and that is needed for the 100 percent automatic and personalized draft of their individual report. For instance, "Is Mrs. X the driver of car Y?" Or, "Is the Dodge Challenger still driven by your CEO?" Every month ask for some additional information. These customers will be happy to provide it because they want to receive a relevant management report to help them better manage their car fleet. This creates a win-win relationship between the company and the end customer, an exchange of business expertise for a better knowledge of each customer. Here again, the automation of individualized consulting creates added value for the customer but does not destroy jobs.

Gains obtained:

- You build a database rich in statistics that your marketing team can make the most of to sell additional services.
- You finally see the ROI from your CRM.
- Your customers appreciate this consulting service, which your competitors do not know how to provide.
- At the time of contract renewal, you have automatically

collected so much information on the use patterns of your rented vehicles that you are the only company able to make a well-argued, suitable financial proposal. And you can thereby justify a potentially higher cost than your competitors.

AI technologies used: RPA and expert system.
Configuration or setup time for an MVP: Sixty human days plus data integration into your CRM.
Types of data or elements used and produced: At the input of each monthly questionnaire, the data is structured; at the output, the recommendation provided is individualized expertise. If the one-page document you send contains a summary of the fleet situation, this part is natural language information.

Scenario 3: Appointment Management

Your activity requires many appointments with external contacts, which is time consuming. AI can help you automate this repetitive task.

Description of the automation solution: Plug-and-play solutions, such as Clara Labs, x.ai, and Julie Desk, exist to take over and manage email exchanges with your contacts. They also can find a suitable date on two or more calendars and in several languages.

Gains obtained:

• Time savings of nearly an hour per day for each employee whose planner includes about five to six internal or external daily appointments.

• Flexibility in the case of unforeseen events, as the system takes over to reschedule your appointments.

AI technologies used: RPA with NLU, system expert, and NLG.
Configuration or setup time: One week.
Types of data or elements used and produced: The exchange of information regarding an appointment is typically natural language information.

Scenario 4: Predictive Maintenance

Your business involves designing, distributing, and deploying industrial goods for your customers. You equip them with more and more sensors and smart-connected objects that collect data on the site use of your products. When connected to the internet, these devices are part of a market named the Internet of Things (IoT). With the client's consent, you can analyze this information using AI to predict potential failures. One such application is predictive maintenance.

Description of the automation solution: Predictive maintenance, based on ML, consists of using AI to analyze data and to determine any correlation between symptoms that appear ahead of breakdowns. These can then be anticipated, allowing for early intervention before any potential problem develops for your customers. But such a solution cannot be applied overnight. A significant database (about two years' worth of data collection, depending on case differences) must be collected for this predictive technology to function as expected. The goal is to proactively automate troubleshooting instead of scheduling repeat maintenance visits.

Gains obtained:

- Drastic reduction in the number of breakdowns, thanks to preemptive maintenance.
- Better management of spare parts inventory.
- Less troubleshooting needed at night and on weekends.

AI technologies used: ML. The most important part of the data preparation work has to be done using dedicated tools that are not directly related to AI.

Configuration and setup time: It is probably a full-time project for a few people, if you take into account the entire data collection, storage, and analysis processes.

Types of data or elements used and produced: High-quality structured data because there is no human intervention involved in its collection by the sensor, its storage in the database, and its analysis and correlation found in the collected data.

Scenario 5: Meeting Reports

Following an appointment with an internal or external customer, your job requires you to write a complete meeting summary in which a predefined set of information must be included.

Description of the automation solution: Whether it involves on-site visits, meetings, or phone calls, 90 percent of the work can be done without touching the keyboard. Software installed on a computer, smartphone, or tablet reasons on the customer data and the nature of the work in progress. From there, the software asks close-ended questions to which the user responds by checking answers on a multiple-choice list or by shifting a cursor with the mouse or a finger on a touch screen. The goal is to automate the writing of meeting reports, often a repetitive task.

Gains obtained:

- Decreased time spent writing reports by a factor of ten.
- Each answer is good-quality structured data.
- The spelling is perfect, and AI will know to reread the report contents in the future if necessary (for instance, for comparison or monitoring purposes).

AI technologies used: Business rules engine, such as system expert and NLG.

Configuration or setup time: About forty human days.

Types of data or elements used and produced: The reports are typically commentaries or statement summaries, thus natural language information. But if the reports include recommendations, then it is individualized expertise.

Scenario 6: Augmented Reality and Artificial Intelligence

Strictly speaking, augmented reality and virtual reality are not AI. Though together these two technologies can automate service processes, which was still hard to imagine just a few years ago. The following example, based on a real-life use case, is a mixed scenario that uses both AI and augmented reality. It summarizes the future of selling clothes online to show how AI can automate the selection and production of unique goods.

Description of the automation solution: Imagine that you are looking for something to wear to a wedding. The system (based online) will ask you about your preferences and for your measurements. It compares your needs to market trends (this is where ML comes in) to offer you several choices of currently fashionable clothing and accessories that match your taste. Before ordering, thanks to augmented reality software installed on your smartphone, you can see yourself in your new outfit on a photo or video. This also enables you to share your potential outfits with your friends via messages or social media and ask for their opinions.

AI Supporting Custom-Made Production With a B2C Purchase Example

The ability to create a unique dress at a ready to wear price becomes the #1 purchase criterion.

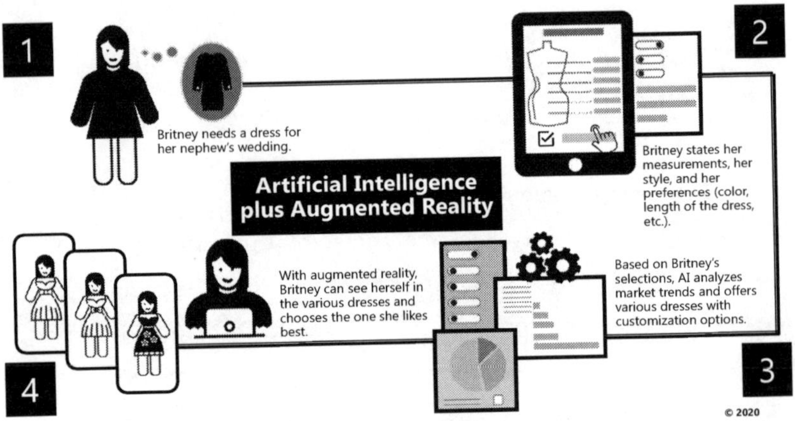

Gains obtained:

- The ability to actually create a unique custom-made outfit.
- No price barriers. The budget is stated from the start, and the outfit is put together taking the budget into consideration.
- The ability to easily consult friends for their opinions before the purchase.

AI technologies used: ML and AR.

Configuration and setup time for an MVP: Plus or minus one hundred human days.

Types of data or elements used and produced: At the input of the questionnaire, data is structured; at the output, the images are raw data. The final order is structured data.

Finally, probably one of the biggest mistakes made in business these past decades involving the internet's influence, among others, has been to try to fully automate business processes. While automating 80 percent of a task is almost always simple and affordable, automating 100 percent of a task is very difficult, if not impossible. Michael Hafner, head of Mercedes-Benz's autopilot research and development (R&D) department, describes his job: "We have learned that the development of these [automation] systems is a bit like climbing a mountain. The first few feet from the base station to the summit seems easy. But the closer you come to the goal, the more rarefied the atmosphere becomes, the more strength is required for each further step, and the more complex the challenges you have to resolve." The constraints that apply to the design of a car autopilot do apply, to some degree, to the automation of any task. That's why cobots, covered in the next chapter, represent the safest approach to a successful AI deployment.

More generally, fully understanding the type of data available in your company, and the differences between raw and structured data, natural language data (information), knowledge, and individualized expertise is key to efficiently using AI in the service sector. It's also critical in defining how AI will change your market sector's business model, knowing that it's better to understand it before your competitors actually apply it. If providing intellectual services—namely, human expertise—is the basis of your business model, you should understand how AI's automation of individualized expertise can change your market. If you provide knowledge or information to your customers via electronic communications, you will need to provide what really interests them: individualized expertise. In this context, collaborative AI to automate part of the workload represents a real disruption that will affect the way you market, sell, communicate, and provide technical and commercial support to your customers as well as provide an incredible opportunity for all those who seize it early on.

3.

Cobot or AI That Augments Human Intelligence

Two-thirds of employees would trust a robot boss more than a real one.

AI at Work Study[18]

18 "New Study: 64% of People Trust a Robot More Than Their Manager," Oracle, October 15, 2019, http://www.oracle.com/corporate/pressrelease/robots-at-work-101519.html.

Artificial intelligence opens new avenues for service activities by redefining the computing of tomorrow, notably through language management and machine learning. It seems that more and more repetitive tasks, once only performed by knowledge workers, can now be automated by software. However, the technical challenges to achieve this are tremendous, and it will take years for many of the automated tasks that involve reasoning or language to yield comprehensive results. More often than not, AI only partially automates a task that then requires human intervention to validate or amend the result, using human common sense, empathy, and creativity. To cover a broad spectrum of applications in service activities, we must shift your ambitions for AI from hoping it will replace human workers to hoping it can augment your workforce. AI must help knowledge workers in a different way by supporting them and increasing their day-to-day work skills. This takes the form of a collaborative robot, or cobot, which we will describe in detail in this chapter.

You Already Use a Cobot Every Day

The car GPS was the first digital cobot to be mass deployed. It perfectly illustrates the first-generation cobots that we'll all be using tomorrow in our companies: It analyzes millions of traffic-related data points to suggest a route based on the priority parameters selected by the user in a graphic form and a limited oral script. It becomes a digital copilot and allows the sharing of tasks between people and machines. The driver focuses on driving, not on choosing the fastest, cheapest, or shortest route. Many drivers use their GPS even when they know the route well because it can analyze traffic congestion in real time and suggest an alternate route before they can detect the traffic issue themselves. But the ability of the GPS to communicate with the driver in natural language is still limited. We would like the GPS to explain why it is telling us to change routes from the planned one and what the differences are, for instance, in terms of tolls, driving comfort, and fuel consumption. We can then choose whether or not to follow its suggestion. In this sense, the GPS is a first-generation cobot that does not augment its user's intelligence. Its ability to generate intelligent language is still too limited, yet there's no doubt that this feature will be added soon. Even those die-hard people who thought they knew the road better than their GPS did recognize today that the machine is still much more accurate in the vast majority of cases.

AI Serving the Employee: The Cobot

Today, AI has some clear technical limits, yet the fear of people being replaced by machines on some tasks remains a psychological deterrent. Cobots overcome this human psychological challenge by making people's lives easier at work and helping them accomplish more and at a higher quality than before. A cobot is a sort of a knowledge conveyor that is quickly accepted by employees and augments their performance, driving value for the business.

As the twenty-first century progresses, the power of AI provides an effective answer to the four constraints on companies described in chapter 1:

1. Too much collected and available data, which limits an individual's ability to analyze the large volumes of information.
2. A wealth of product or service offerings, which makes it difficult, if not impossible, to determine the best product that matches the needs of an internal or external customer.
3. The number of regulations and internal business rules to process, which exceeds the reasoning capabilities of the human brain and consequently heightens the risk of flawed consulting and potential legal liability.
4. Customers or prospects are increasingly better educated through the internet, which convinces them that their own problem analyses are accurate. They become demanding, wanting immediate answers at ever-lower prices.

Distribution of Roles between Employee and Cobot

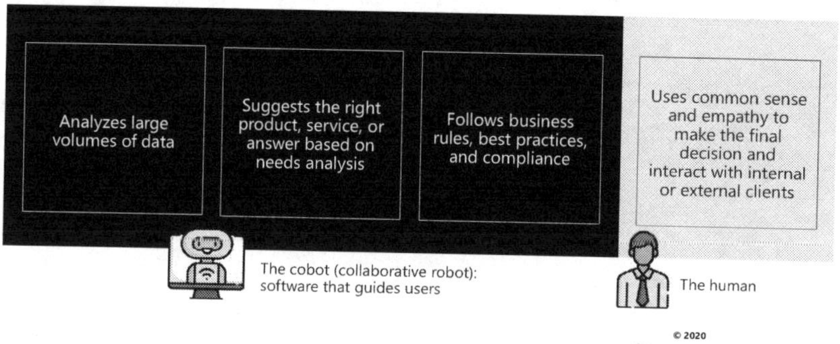

Cobots process the first three of the constraints that knowledge workers face on the job today, and the knowledge worker steps in for the fourth:

- Data analysis: This is necessary for dealing with any situation. A cobot processes hundreds or thousands of data points instantly.
- Proposals: These are based on an understanding of the customer's request and the company's available offers and resources. In a logical and automatic way, a cobot connects the expressed needs to the multitude of available products or services and offers the knowledge worker the best available solutions.
- Possible solutions: These are filtered to align with the company's business rules, best practices, and regulatory compliance and to offer the most relevant recommendation for the internal or external customer.
- The knowledge worker: The human step that applies common sense, relational and emotional intelligence, and creativity to moderate the cobot's logic, which to a human would otherwise be construed as cold.

The term *cobot* (collaborative robot) comes from the world of industrial production.[19] As the name suggests, it is a robot that works in collaboration with humans. A cobot in the service sector takes the form of a PC, tablet, or smartphone software that communicates with an employee using a voice interface, a touch screen, or a keyboard. A cobot seamlessly guides a knowledge worker through this communication process, and its existence may or may not be known to the end customer who may just think they are getting stellar customer service. Technically, the cobot reasons without a decision tree, enabling faster processing, easier upkeep, and quicker development.

Therefore, a cobot has four specific characteristics:

1. It knows how to reason based on a large volume of data, which itself is based on codified business rules.
2. It knows how to interact intelligently with an employee in natural language, **asking close-ended questions** just like a human expert would.
3. It relies on the company's knowledge (which is codified in business rules) to produce individualized expertise in the form of personalized and well-argued responses based on each specific context.
4. It automates a significant portion of administrative tasks so that the user of a cobot keeps using it, even when they know how to handle an issue without it.

---

19 *Cobot was coined by J. Edward Colgate and Michael Peshkin in 1996. They described their Cobot in their 1997 patent as an industrial term: "an apparatus and method for direct physical interaction between a person and a general-purpose manipulator controlled by a computer."*

To fit the definition of a cobot, a software should be able to do the following:

• Summarize a situation in natural language from a reasoning process based on structured data, which in turn comes from the information system (CRM, ERP, data warehouse, etc.) or external databases.

• Make a diagnosis to explain which processes are compatible or incompatible with the best business practices.

• Suggest recommendations, explaining in natural language why they are appropriate for each unique context. The knowledge worker amends the suggestions by applying their common sense, creativity, and empathy.

• Automate 80 percent of repetitive and administrative tasks, such as visit reports, thank-you emails summarizing the call, propagating the CRM, technical reports, or price quotations.

Cobots therefore differ from chatbots whose responses are at an information or knowledge level, not at the expertise level. In the past, chatbots were a kind of search engine with a friendly user interface that seeked answers in prewritten FAQs. Google's search engine, for example, is not a cobot but is much closer to a generic chatbot, searching vast numbers of prewritten pieces of information that may or may not be relevant for the searcher. If you do not know how to formulate a specific question with the proper vocabulary, you cannot find what you are looking for. Technically, most chatbots do not reason on information system data, do not know how to ask intelligent questions relevant to a given context, and do not produce a reasoned answer.

Cobots produce individualized expertise or eventually guide users through a process. They use close-ended questions, not simulated natural language processing (NLP). Chatbots try to guess what the user has said or written. The user interface of a cobot is less friendly, but the close-ended question approach is a more efficient and professional path to solve complex issues. Cobots are targeted toward employees when chatbots based on NLP are generally deployed for customers or users asking basic questions.

Cobots must know how to augment the information system (ERP or CRM depending on the context) with all the collected data, including anything related to problems encountered while improving the quality of the company's overall processes. Cobots will relieve knowledge workers of their administrative reporting tasks concerning what has been done, how, and why. These characteristics will incentivize an employee to continue using cobots, even when they are confident that they already know the best answer or the best procedure without the assistance of their new favorite tool.

A cobot is a virtual expert that aims to boost the users' level of expertise and efficiency. It is the knowledge workers' second brain. A logical one.

The Different Types of Cobots

By 2025, companies will be able to equip themselves with two types of cobots: the generic and the proprietary. As a service, the generic cobots, made available by suppliers of hardware, computer software, or other tools used at work, will become mandatory for manufacturers, and their efficiency will become a key point in the buyer's decision process. Proprietary cobots, adapted to department operations, will be specific to each company and will model the core business of each department.

Generic cobots will download to your smartphone, computer, or tablet, just as easily as you download an application today. For example, legal solutions publishers will offer you access to their cobots for a pay-per-use fee or for a certain duration of use (subscription with unlimited use during the established period). So when you have a question about how you can protect your intellectual property during a conversation with a potential foreign competitor, the cobot may ask you to gather enough information for a comprehensive reasoning on the subject of intellectual property, just as a lawyer would. The cobot may ask you who you are, how your contact competes with you, what product you're competing against, why you have to talk to the competitor, and so on. From each answer, without a predefined path, the cobot will determine the next question, sometimes explaining why it is asking you that question in particular. At the end of the questioning, the cobot will draw up a contract in your contact's language—that is, a truly personalized confidentiality agreement you may submit to your contact to protect yourself from any potential theft of your knowledge. These cobots as a service open up potential for exciting new markets. For example, we can easily imagine app stores for expertise in which users pay to download knowledge for their cobots. However, these applications will by nature of their mass availability remain fairly generic and will address small businesses or private customers.

Company cobots, meanwhile, will centralize all the internal knowledge and know-how. The business rules used as the basis for cobot reasoning are those defined internally by experienced employees whom we will call experts. A company cobot embeds the modeling of internal knowledge, whether it is technical, marketing, sales, or related to the customer relationship. This knowledge already exists within any company, formally or informally. It can be found in training manuals, product or service manuals, the company's website FAQs, and the experts' memories. These experts know, for instance, that when a customer asks for a specific service, they must ask certain specific questions to better understand the request and to submit a coherent sales proposal in return. Or that when a customer calls for technical support for a particular product, they must define how it is being used to better understand the cause of the problem. With cobots, reasoning is automatically rerun after each answer provided by the customer, thus allowing the cobot to seamlessly understand a customer context and to offer the best expert advice to the customer. Once the context is understood, a cobot will summarize the situation and explain the advice offered (and why) in a few lines. No more rigid decision-making trees forcing customers down predefined paths, and no more question overload with useless or incoherent questions aimed at weary customers.

Cobots have the potential to revolutionize consulting businesses, and many companies are already developing proprietary cobots. Up until now, consultants took their know-how with them when they left a company, but with cobots, valuable knowledge can be retained and stay accessible. Cobots represent the first dynamic knowledge management tool that remains the property of the company. They can render contextual the static knowledge base of any business.

The Challenge of Deploying Cobots

Cobots have not been previously deployed mostly for technological and public perception reasons, including the following:

• Conventional computing does not know how to converse. At best, a computer program can offer what we ironically call a bidirectional monologue, where the user asks a question and the computer answers but is unable to ask the user an enlightened question in return. Intelligent dialogue means that both parties are able to ask intelligent questions (without a predefined script), understand them, and respond without preprogrammed answers.

• Technologies that could automate intelligent dialogue were not available two years ago. Today, interesting AI-based solutions that approach human dialogue do exist, such as Clevy.io, but they come from recent start-ups, while the market has not yet caught on to the huge progress cobots have made in the automation of services. Yet it is now perfectly feasible to make a first cobot (or MVP of a cobot) in less than one hundred human days.

• To write a custom-made, personalized, and succinct answer (as opposed to one based on a predefined template), you may need NLG software that can write like a human being. This AI technology is now available from several software companies.

• These technologies are not mastered or marketed by GAFA, so the media doesn't focus on this matter.

• Adoption of cobots requires change in management across the enterprise. A project manager in charge of setting up a cobot must redefine the division of tasks between machine and employee. It is an organizational obstacle that requires the involvement of general management and therefore takes time.

Companies Augmented by Cobots

The ongoing collaborative AI revolution is facilitated by cobots that bring at least five significant changes to this sector:

1. Services become an industrial good: All companies have more or less important service activities (sales, marketing, technical support, consulting, training, etc.). Whether invoicing is based on the sale of products or services, the viability of a company always depends on the quality of the organization and its employees. The more the final product becomes consulting, the more the individual quality of the person who delivers the service becomes important. In addition, the business models of companies that don't sell products are linked to the gross margin

between the sale price of the service and the wage cost (and possibly the depreciation of the work tool). Traditionally, when employees in service activities leave a company, they take their know-how with them and can become competitors. With AI-based cobots, service companies have to be managed just like companies that develop an industrial product. Their knowledge bases and their data are intellectual property, materialized and identifiable, that remains in the company and can possibly become sellable products in their own right.

2. Cobots disrupt the services business model: There is no longer any need for an expert to deliver a service in person. Potentially, the gross margin and the sales revenue become almost equal if AI produces the consulting service without resorting to sought-after, expensive human experts for help. R&D of the knowledge base and data may represent a large investment, but when it works well, it reduces the cost of service production.

3. Cobots allow for services at scale globally: A company equipped with cobots is able to promote its services on a large scale, and, perhaps in no time, on an international one. The marketing or sales team no longer targets only the local market based on the availability of consultants to deliver the service and limited by the distance between prospects and customers, but it can also provide services on a global scale because the advice is digitized.

4. Cobots drive higher valuations in the services sector: The valuation of a company that has industrialized its expertise by using cobots will increase sharply. Traditionally, a service company is valued based on the last six months—or at best the last eighteen months—of its sales revenue. Well-functioning corporate cobots demonstrate that knowledge can be industrialized and prove that the service sector's business model is scalable, meaning that the doubling of sales has no significant operational consequences. Thus, the valuation of the service company could double, triple, or even increase tenfold. A company's prospective buyer no longer acquires an existing customer base or inherits an existing sales revenue but rather a market potential and intellectual property materialized by cobots and business rules.

5. Cobots disrupt the services pricing model: An expert is typically invoiced on the basis of time spent. If 80 percent of his expertise is transferred to a cobot, then time is no longer the fixed factor that determines the cost of a service delivery. Of course, the remaining 20 percent that represents the noble work will be billed according to time spent and at a high price. With a cobot, the pricing policy of a service is related to the added value that the service brings rather than to its cost of production (time) as in a traditional model.

Rarely has a computer tool brought companies so much exceptional added value and high margins in the short term.

Employees Augmented and Freed by Cobots

Cobots bring about several major positive changes in the life of companies, in particular in the life of employees. The nature of their work changes, and their perception of cobots is positive.

In the same way that a GPS changed the way you plan a trip and drive, a cobot changes the perception of the day's work. The tasks required of knowledge workers tend to become more interesting, more high-end, and different in nature:

• AI increasingly assists knowledge workers: The limits of the human brain are no longer an obstacle, and apprehension about an expanded work environment is no longer a cause of stress. As a result, with a cobot's help, knowledge workers become proficient in a wider range of products and services, and businesses can make more and more offers that are more sophisticated and above all more personalized, tailored to the needs of each client.

• Employees focus on noble work: In many cases, the employee becomes cocreator of the product or service built with the cobot as custom made becomes the new rule, without any additional cost over mass production. Offering a customized service is noble work that provides a lot of professional satisfaction. By analyzing data and validating the business rules and conformity of the proposal submitted, a cobot is key to providing many internal and external customers with this type of value creation.

- Cobots foster more human interaction: With a cobot, an employee can focus primarily on communicating with the client, using relational and emotional intelligence to better understand their human contact. The employee's knowledge of the technical nature of offers, professional practices, or applicable legislation is less needed because it is essentially entrusted to a cobot, which applies a rational and exhaustive approach to determine the best response. A knowledge worker intervenes with common sense to confirm or refute a cobot's suggestion. The employee is still the final decision maker and the face of the company but is freed from performing some of the analysis and data-driven repetitive tasks.
- Cobots will usher in a new work environment: Noble work will develop considerably and replace increasingly automated repetitive tasks. This is not to say that cobots will eventually eliminate service activities performed by human beings, as one might think.

Let's go back to our example of a legal contract. If a generic cobot on intellectual property is not available, a company that speaks to a competitor must choose one of three solutions to protect itself:

- Not drafting a contract or talking during the interview with the competitor so as not to reveal any sensitive information.
- Patching together a confidentiality agreement from a contract template found online.
- Asking the company lawyer to draft a custom

contract at a cost of somewhere between two and five hours at his hourly rate.

Most SMEs that do not have in-house legal advice opt for the first solution, even if it entails taking some real risks. Legal departments at large organizations would require weeks to draft a contract. With the availability of a legal cobot at an affordable cost, a company can choose this modern approach: A cobot drafts a custom contract after an individualized questioning phase. Now there's a high probability that the competitor requests a clause revision. The intervention of a human lawyer will therefore be necessary when the issue to address requires common sense and relational intelligence, as, for example, qualifying a bothersome clause. But this noble work service will be less expensive because it will take less time. In fact, by lowering the price of access to such a service, a cobot generates a new source of added-value work for a knowledge worker (the lawyer in our example) and a somewhat consistent source at that, as, most of the time, it is necessary to validate or even finalize the work of a cobot.

The following are some of the ways knowledge workers perceive the cobot as an ally who augments them while also improving their well-being at work:

- Cobots reduce human error: The cobot not only ensures greater efficiency in the decision-making process and the delivery of advice and improved reliability of the proposed result but also frees knowledge workers from daily stress because it collaborates with them, suggests the best solution for any particular context, and significantly decreases their error rate.

• Cobots are on-the-job trainers: The best-designed cobots explain their reasoning logic to knowledge workers for the purpose of continuing education. A cobot not only suggests the best actions and decisions but also explains why they are the best in the user's natural language. It is crucial that a cobot pull the employee upward—that is, help them develop their general knowledge in any given area of expertise—so that they acquire the common sense and judgment necessary to produce quality work. The more a knowledge worker uses a cobot, the more they learn the business rules, the best practices, and the questions to ask to define a customer's request and then match it to the available products and services. We learn better and with less stress when training is tightly linked to practice.

• Cobots upskill the workforce: Cobots boost knowledge workers' areas of expertise to a realm that has been traditionally reserved for experts. When a knowledge worker has to perform a task for which they have no expertise, a cobot communicates with them and guides them through the process. The knowledge worker discovers new and motivating worlds and possibly even new callings.

The use of a cobot will soon become a market requirement when dealing with a service provider. To bring added value to work in a world that is becoming increasingly rich in possibilities and more complex, every knowledge worker needs to be assisted by a cobot. We even predict that in the requests for services and consulting, the originators will ask the respondents about the choice, the qualities, and ultimately the labels and certifications of the cobot they'll use to deliver the service. In the next decade, the quality of any featured cobot will become a determining factor in choosing a service provider. The cobot will become the knowledge worker's second brain.

We are convinced that rather than seeing any competition between AI and employees, we will witness significant gains in efficiency, reliability, and job satisfaction from the collaboration between knowledge workers and AI.

The revolution is the emergence of a human–machine association, which will often take the form of a cobot. It is in this sense that we have renamed "augmented human intelligence" collaborative AI.

Examples of Cobot Use Today

Next you will find a list of five concrete use cases demonstrating that human intelligence augmented by cobots is a reality today and that you can deploy cobots in your own business now. Of course, the given setup times for an initial version of a cobot are estimates because, among other things, the quality of your company's available data may affect the cobot's functionality or require additional preparation work. You can also go to cobot-ai.com to watch a video of a cobot.

Scenario 1: Configuration and Sales Support

You manufacture and install solar panels. About 20 percent of your purchase orders include errors that you will have to resolve during installation because some of your technical sales representatives don't have enough experience. You want to diminish these problems that directly affect your margin and customer satisfaction and thereby increase sales efficiency by 20 percent with an AI solution.

Actions to support salespeople: Create a configuration tool that is based on a few photos of the installation site, and the nature of the support (tile or slate roof, orientation of the house, geographical location, etc.) will question the technical salesperson on their tablet or PC to help them correctly enter the necessary information. The customer-specific questionnaire will be carried out either on-site during a salesperson's visit, online, or on the phone with a call center. It will include questions aimed at better understanding the client's goals. The end solution will be a well-reasoned business proposal that includes the return on investment calculation for the customer.

Gains obtained:

- You have automated your know-how, and your technical sales representatives focus on the customer relationship, not on the technicality of products, options, or their exceptions. Your error rate drops when the solution is in focus.
- Your salespeople increase their number of customer visits

because they spend less time doing administrative work, such as preparing and customizing sales proposals.

• Customers receive an individualized, well-reasoned sales proposal without any spelling errors as soon as they have completed the questionnaire.

• The questionnaire makes it possible to obtain well-structured, quality data. You have collected an incredible amount of data on each customer for your marketing department and for other projects in the future.

AI technologies used: ML, expert system, and NLG.
Configuration and setup time for an MVP: Around fifty human days and the time of an internal expert who really knows the subject matter.

Scenario 2: End Customer Technical Support

You manage rentals at holiday village resorts and have to deal with customer complaints during the peak season when you've hired temporary staff. So you have more work and a summer seasonal staff that is not necessarily well trained and that changes every year. How do you maintain a good level of quality despite these constraints?

Actions to support seasonal workers: Set up a dynamic questionnaire that is based on the configuration of each holiday location, the breakdown history, and the business knowledge of the company and that will perfectly refine the customer's request, dispatch the right employee(s) to best deal with the complexity of the problem, and send the vacationer a summary email that reassures them.

Gains obtained:

- Seasonal workers become quasi-experts without any specific training.
- The degree of urgency is better gauged, as is the choice of the right service provider.
- It is a time-saver because the diagnosis has already been made, and the service provider can arrive on the very first visit with the appropriate spare part in hand. Thus, the overall breakdown time is shortened.
- The solution can be adapted online to provide twenty-four-hour service.
- Customers appreciate receiving a support confirmation email with the description of the problem and are therefore more patient.

AI technologies used: Expert system, NLU, and NLG.
Configuration and setup time for an MVP: Thirty to sixty human days, depending on the complexity.

Scenario 3: Auditing Support

Auditing is your core business, whether to validate the conformity of a good or service or to evaluate damages.

Actions to support your auditors: Set up a cobot—for example, on their smartphone or PC—that will interact with the auditor to guide them. With each answer, the system reevaluates its analysis and raises a new question. There is no decision tree to avoid long and tedious or unnecessary questions. The solution can be a partial one and concern only certain specific types of audits. Senior auditors are in charge of the rules' evolution. As for juniors, the tool allows them to learn faster without making mistakes, much like a GPS that teaches you a new route that hadn't occurred to you.

Gains obtained:

- Excellent audit quality is achieved in terms of both form and substance.
- Once again, the collected data is structured and therefore reusable later.
- Results are generated instantly, saving hours as compared to quality manual writing.
- On average, an AI-supported audit phase can be accomplished 30 percent faster than a manual one. In our example, proof verification is always done manually, but some of it could be automated as well.

AI technologies used: ML, expert system, NLG.
Configuration and setup time for an MVP: Plus or minus sixty human days.

Scenario 4: Cobot-Assisted Customer Service

Your customer service team, which has been in place for several years, is already overwhelmed, and adding new products and services to your portfolio complicates their job and is driving up training costs.

Actions to support customer service: Set up a cobot that does the following:

- Analyzes the tens of thousands of processed and resolved tickets registered from customer calls to build the knowledge base automatically.
- Assists the customer service staff in real time to diagnose the problem faster.
- Supplies the list of definitive and workaround solutions that have been proposed in the past. Eventually, each experienced customer service member will be able to validate the proposed solutions to enrich the quality of the available knowledge base for future use.

Gains obtained:

- Your team focuses on the customer relationship, not the technicality of the product or service that generated their technical support request.
- The duration of support calls is decreased by 30 percent on average.
- New team members improve their professional skills in less than a month.

• The client is satisfied to talk to a support team member whose level of expertise is reliable and who provides solutions quickly.

AI technologies used: ML, NLU, and expert system.
Average Configuration and setup time for an MVP: Fifty human days.

Scenario 5: Smart Recruitment

You are a temporary employment agency. You want to offer your customer service employees a tool that connects a company's needs to available candidates who you have already interviewed and qualified.

Actions to support the account manager: Using software that helps question the client on their needs for the open position, the cobot determines a list of possible candidates by calculating a relevance score. The cobot also clearly lists both the convincing arguments to use for any chosen candidate to accept the position and those for the employer to hire such a well-suited candidate. Any contact with either the employer or the candidate is done with the help of comprehensive reasoning, from which the consultant selects their sales arguments. Based on feedback from the employer and the candidate, the AI tool automatically refines the relevant score calculation. The emotional intelligence component remains at the discretion of the account manager. The goal here is not to produce a perfect final document but rather a draft to be completed by the temporary work agency consultant.

Gains obtained:

- A well-reasoned proposal that matches a candidate's qualifications to a client's needs while accruing profits for the recruiting company and that is four times more likely to be accepted than a proposal based on reading a résumé alone.
- The customer is pleased to speak to a sales team with a reliable level of competence and who is quick to offer a solution.

AI technologies used: Expert system, NLG, and ML for relevance score.

Configuration and setup time: Plus or minus forty human days, depending on the number of criteria.

We can state that AI-based augmentation of humans in the work environment, not their replacement, will become AI's most obvious and promising field of application over the next decade. Hundreds of companies have already deployed cobots, as previously described, and report great satisfaction with having done so. Returns on investment are rapid while many companies have also experienced gains in quality and efficiency.

Employees are generally enthusiastic, as the need for concentration on their daily tasks is alleviated, while their attention to those tasks that require human intelligence is increased, and the quality of their work is improved.

The services sector revolution begins with cobots, one of the pillars of collaborative AI. Beyond the automation of tasks mentioned in chapter 2 and the power of cobots, AI will also revolutionize business marketing. We've already had a preview of this upcoming transformation in advertising, today dominated by GAFA, thanks to AI. Let's further explore collaborative AI's fields of application to marketing in our companies.

4.

AI-Augmented Marketing

By 2022, 30% of organizations will use explainable AI to build trust.[20]

Rita Sallam, Distinguished VP Analyst at Gartner

---

20 *At the annual Gartner Symposium for CIOs in the fall of 2019, held in Barcelona.*

Augmented marketing is the third component of collaborative AI. It is also one of the simplest ways to launch an initial artificial intelligence project within a company, since marketing teams are traditionally familiar with data manipulation. AI brings at least four major transformations to any business: true one-to-one marketing, individualized and explicit marketing arguments, no-limit marketing, and predictive analysis. This new AI approach can also help build a positive and memorable brand with a limited budget.

Before getting into the details of these four use cases of AI in marketing, it is important to point out that a marketing manager must distinguish among three types of structured data:

1. Administrative data: Data with limited marketing interest. For instance, the contact's last name, first name, email address, credit card number, and the like says almost nothing about who the customer is or how best to offer them added value to a project or service.

2. Usage data: This type of data is fundamental for marketing teams because it reveals customer habits, such as how a customer drives, where they go on vacation and with whom, whether they have a dog or a cat, what kind of books they read, and so on. It's usage data, when connected to the core business, that enables efficient marketing. It brings

value to both the customer and the company. We will see later how to collect usage data.

3. Customer action data: With all the focus on guessing what customers might want based on marketing profiles and other information, it is easy for marketers to forget that customers often show us what they are looking for. This can take the form of actions taken on your website (content downloaded, pages viewed, etc.), but it can also take the form of questions the customer has asked of your sales team.

One-to-One Marketing

The holy grail of marketing has always been one-to-one. With this approach, each customer is treated in a unique way regardless of whether they belong to any given market segment. Conventional marketing efforts attempt to build customer profiles and then guess what the customer might want or what they might be looking for. AI completely shifts the paradigm: you can not only ask the customer what they are looking for but also communicate with them in a 100 percent one-to-one approach. The service offered and the answers provided are therefore custom made and truly adapted to each customer's needs. This is already the norm in certain trades. For example, in luxury hotels, employees learn the name of each and every guest staying at the hotel and remember their favorite breakfast drink from their second day. This is possible since their numbers are manageable but becomes more difficult when the business grows and the customer relationship is less direct, without systematic physical contact. Traditionally, to achieve such a degree of connection, marketing departments of large B2C companies divide customers into profiles based on criteria such as age, type of products ordered, purchasing power, and so on. If you are an SME and have few B2B customers, you know all their names as well as their buying and bargaining habits. That is indeed traditional one-to-one marketing and possible in small organizations. This approach is an expensive one and is limited by the memory capacity of the human brain. But it is essential because it humanizes the customer-supplier relationship and thus forges solid, sustainable connections. For the supplier, it is the most effective way to make the customer forget the very existence of competition.

How can you automate this one-to-one approach when the company sells in B2C or when the number of customers reaches levels that prevent them from being individually recognized, even in the department in charge of customer relations?

AI analyzes each customer's data to suggest the best logic-based decision. More precisely, each customer becomes their own market segment. The customer becomes unique and is treated individually. They are not denied anything as long as they're willing to pay for the service. Each communication is personalized to the customer's context, while AI suggests or determines what to write or say, what advice to give, and which product or service to sell, regardless of the channel (email, SMS, mail, phone). Whatever the size of your business, thanks to AI, marketing's holy grail becomes attainable for all, and the notion of market segment disappears.

The benefits of this approach are a high-quality service and a much higher conversion rate from each marketing contact to a sale. We will illustrate how AI enables a successful one-to-one marketing approach in a use case described later in this chapter.

Individualized and Explicit Marketing Arguments

If without further explanation your favorite car mechanic or dealer insists that the best car for you is an electric model, you may be skeptical. But if they explain their reasoning, then it might be easier to convince you. For example, they might tell you that the Tesla is the car you need because you would save $250 per month on gas driving to your office, which is twenty-five miles from your home. They might explain that charging the battery will not be a problem because you live in a detached house with a garage and that such autonomy will facilitate your weekday round-trip commute, as you'll only need to recharge on weekends. By explaining the reasoning, your mechanic is much more likely to convince you to follow their advice. That's what good salespeople do intuitively.

Before AI, this individualized, rationalized approach was possible only on a small scale with human contact (whether face-to-face or on the phone) and required that the salesperson know the prospective buyer well. Sales in any business field, and for each interaction, always require a first phase of listening to the customer's needs and understanding their habits. Good salespeople ask lots of questions in the first phase, whereas bad salespeople talk at their potential customers.

The one-to-one marketing approach can determine the content of the message and possibly select which proposal to offer the customer based on what they have just bought or on their profile. However, individualized sales argumentation goes further, explicitly presenting the characteristics of the chosen product or service as benefits.

AI, or more precisely a combination of AI technologies, makes it possible to automate the argumentation process. AI doesn't invent anything but rather is ultimately based on the best sales approach you have chosen or applied, perhaps from an analysis of your customers' historical data. Instead of simply offering an adapted product or service at a certain price, you clearly explain to the customer why the proposed offer corresponds exactly to their needs. To render a line of argument even more effective, and to build trust with the customer, AI can explain the limits of the offer. This approach also makes it possible to offer two different versions of a product or service: one at a competitive price point and another at a more premium rate. The automated sales argumentation explains the limitations of the first offer to the customer and highlights the benefits of acquiring a product or service in a higher range or buying additional options. Whichever approach is selected, AI makes it possible to automate individualized and explicit argumentation. The application examples described later showcase this solution's tremendous added value. Sales people are still needed to add common sense and creativity to the output of the solution.

Any line of argument will be more effective if you have quality data—not only administrative data but also, and more importantly, usage and customer action data that is related to the potential buyer's lifestyle and immediate need. Even if you're not ready to deploy a collaborative AI solution, it's important to ask yourself today what types of data you collect and how.

Automated sales argumentation should probably be one of the priority applications to deploy in any company for a critical reason: statistically, a customer is about four times more likely to make a purchase when the offer is built around a personalized proposal that is explicitly argued. This suggests an incredible return on investment for your business.

No-Limit Marketing

Marketing teams' leeway is often limited by sales teams. Based on their knowledge of a market's trends and its evolution, marketers want to create new, differentiated, and high-margin offers, which salespeople rarely appreciate. Salespeople, on the other hand, are often reluctant to learn about new services or products, their positioning, the qualification questions to ask their contacts, and the appropriate argumentation because to do all this requires substantial effort. As we mentioned in chapter 1 in the section Too Much Information Kills Information, George A. Miller demonstrated the limits of our brains and therefore the great challenge facing sales teams who bear the weight of a large catalog of offers. The more sophisticated a service or product, the more complex it is to fully know. But from a marketing team's point of view, novelty allows differentiation with regard to the competition and therefore often generates an important margin. The price becomes less important than the uniqueness of the offer and its conformity to the customer's needs.

No-limit marketing is an approach where marketers are given carte blanche to create as many products or services as they feel are relevant based on their knowledge of consumers, market trends, and opportunities. In exchange for this freedom, marketers commit to provide rules for the collaborative AI system, rules that link the customers' expressed needs and the offers' characteristics so that AI can automate the selection process and explain why the service offering fits a client's needs. Other rules also ensure that recommendations comply with internal best practices or regulations. They feed the central knowledge database of the company, and all applications (cobot or other) rely on this basis of rules. Thus, in this context, AI plays the role of knowledge conveyor between the marketing team and the sales representatives. Then adding a new product or service to the catalog usually no longer requires specific sales team training because the cobot suggests the best offer that matches each customer's needs and explains why to the salesperson in natural language. The complexity of services offered no longer impedes sales, and salespeople no longer oppose the exponential expansion of their catalog of offers.

This point is fundamental, for instance, during an external growth phase. The idea of combining two companies hoping that one plus one will equal two sometimes evaporates at the door of the sales office. You can have the best messaging, positioning, and differentiation in the world, but if the sales team isn't using it, then what's the point? Without a marketing tool to augment the sales force, it is often just wishful thinking to expect any sales revenue growth due to an increased range of products or services.

Reconciling the marketing and sales teams is the main objective of this no-limit approach made possible by collaborative AI. But it also solves the problematic linear ratio of number of products or services to sales revenue generated. With no-limit marketing based on AI, the more your salespeople offer a wide range of products or services, the more revenue they generate.

Develop a Positive Brand with Collaborative AI

As far as marketing is concerned, a company brand should influence a customer's choice of a product or service. It is based on at least two factors: trust and reputation. The latter is easy to measure. On the other hand, trust is abstract, long to build, and difficult to evaluate. It is a crucial element of success and what justifies a premium price to the consumer, both for B2C and B2B.

Only two types of brand positioning will survive by 2030: The low-cost market and the premium brand (high-end, higher margin).

The low-cost market: The most famous low-cost brand, Walmart, is now almost synonymous with *low cost* in US retail space. In Europe, you have low-cost airlines like EasyJet and Ryanair and low-cost mobile solutions like Free Mobile. These companies have all built their brands in a low-price, high-volume market.

The premium brand: Unlike luxury brands, which represent a market based on scarcity (often by means of artificially high prices), *premium* is a label based on positioning where price tends to become secondary. It may be significantly higher than that of a similar general product or service, but it is the value perceived by the customer that is put forward. In premium services with AI-automated production and a negligible marginal cost, the price of the service depends on what the customer is willing to pay for it, not its cost of production. *Premium* does not prohibit mass production.

A premium product or service is characterized by at least one additional significant benefit when compared to general or even low-cost ones. It can be the company's ability to provide a truly custom-made product or service. The goal of high-quality personalization is not only to make the offer difficult for the customer to compare to others but also to provide a clear added value for which they are ready to pay a higher price. Nike's personalization of shoes is a good example of a premium approach, as each pair becomes potentially unique in the world. This approach is also well adapted to services and impossible to deploy without AI.

Another benefit could be impeccable and individualized one-to-one communication around the product or service. It is not always the product that is exceptional but rather the experience of the service that goes with it. This alone impresses the customer and justifies a slightly higher price. Each interaction with the customer is a communication that goes over what was said, established, or done. Each point is individually covered to explain the value of the premium service, the why, and the how. This approach requires AI.

A premium product or service is also characterized by the fact that it is easy to buy. Companies often make the mistake of focusing on making the good or service easy to sell, with a marketing approach geared toward generating maximum sales revenue for each offer. The right attitude is to change seats and put yourself in the customer's shoes, asking one good question: How do I make my product or service so easy to buy that potential customers don't even consider my competitors anymore? This is the winning strategy adopted by Jeff Bezos for his Amazon Web Services. Over a decade, while IT application hosting services were not Amazon's core business, Amazon Web Services became the global leader in cloud services and now holds almost half of the global market.[21] How? By making the configuration of a remote server as easy as child's play thanks to automation and AI, thus enabling customers to set it up themselves. That is to say, Amazon upset this market by offering an easy-to-buy cloud solution.

The most striking recent example of a premium product is Apple. An iPhone cost about $500 a decade ago. Today, the latest models cost an average of $1,300! For most electronics, prices traditionally fall as sales volumes increase. This is the case for TVs, where the average price continues to drop. Apple did the exact opposite by creating an increasingly premium brand, adding important functions, making its items easy to buy and also easy to use, never requiring the buyer to read the slightest documentation (as opposed to Blackberry).

Another example of this premium approach is Harley-Davidson motorcycles. Harley bikes aren't known for their

21 *"Gartner Says Worldwide IaaS Public Cloud Services Market Grew 31.3% in 2018," Newsroom Press Releases, Gartner, July 29, 2019, http://www.gartner.com/en/newsroom/press-releases/2019-07-29-gartner-says-worldwide-iaas-public-cloud-services-market-grew-31point3-percent-in-2018.*

superior technical performance or even reliability. However, by buying a Harley-Davidson, you are entering a premium club of Harley riders, and you can expect a premium level of support from the Harley-Davidson dealership. Harley-Davidson takes the time to know who their customers are in a way that other companies can only dream of, and the service and community they have created is what makes their product so successful and justifies the higher price tag.

AI is one of the most important drivers for companies wishing to develop their brand. Moreover, both clients and prospective customers perceive adoption of AI positively. This is especially important with a premium positioning that requires highly personalized communication and an individualized argumentation to present its value. Also, AI enables an easy-to-buy approach, as the product or service adjusts itself to each customer's needs automatically. The AI-automated production of individualized expertise (customized consulting and answers) and intelligent communication with each customer help build confidence in the brand. AI collaborates with knowledge workers to provide perfect personalized services even though automated.

The strength of a brand is an element that sets a company apart from its competition. In the eyes of the consumer, brands bring perceived added value to a product or service. Buying a brand-name product or service decreases the perceived risk of making a bad purchase (perhaps incorrectly). The benefits of a strong brand are well established, and AI can develop yours without huge marketing and advertising costs.

Predictive Marketing

Predictive analysis is one of the areas where the use of AI is the most developed. It involves analyzing data (including statistics) to develop predictions about customers' behaviors and to anticipate their future actions, among other things. This predictive approach is also referred to as big data, because large volumes of data are needed to obtain interesting results. In a nutshell, predictive marketing analyzes past actions to anticipate future ones. In the past, companies used data mining technologies. With AI, more specifically machine learning and deep learning approaches based on neural network technology, finding correlations among apparently independent factors is much more powerful. In practice, predictive marketing is particularly effective at detecting global market trends, foreseeing future customer behavior, and determining a development strategy in line with the evolution of demographic data, for instance. At the tactical level, the goal is to suggest the best possible offers at the best time and through the most appropriate communication channel—for example, anticipating losing a customer to the competition and acting proactively to retain them.

Predictive marketing is complementary to one-to-one marketing because the former provides a body of statistical information (without any certainty), whereas the latter uses deterministic reasoning based on each customer's individual data to communicate with them in a precise and rigorously exact way. We will not dwell on possible predictive marketing solutions because many predeveloped offers exist, depending on a company's activity sector. On the other hand, even if predictive marketing is not on your business's agenda, it is important to collect data today, especially usage data, in anticipation of a future investment in this area.

The following are six use cases specifically targeted at B2B or B2C marketing teams.

Scenario 1: Individualized Communications to Each Customer

Your marketing department sends monthly newsletters to your customers and prospects via several channels (email, SMS, messaging apps, etc.) to keep them informed, reinforce credibility, and encourage them to buy new products. The technology you use is an external service or one integrated with your marketing automation platform that allows you to personalize each communication with a gapped sentence approach and to manage the monthly mailing's subscriptions and cancellations. The content of the mail differs depending on the identified profile of each customer. The conversion rate into a purchase is very low, only about 1 percent:

Description of the modern marketing solution: With AI, you can improve this process in three ways: Machine learning allows you to automate the offering of products or services based on purchases from customers of the same profile. This approach is similar to that of Amazon's famous recommendation engine that guides you toward complementary products. Provided that what you sell is not critical and won't generate manifest customer dissatisfaction in case of error or even create a legal risk for your company, the statistical—therefore approximate—machine learning choice is effective.

You can add deterministic rules, previously established by your marketing department, to favor selective offers depending on your customer's equipment.

NLG (text generation) lets you include an individualized argument in your mailings, based on the customer's data, to explain to a customer why this particular product or service is well adapted to their needs.

Gains obtained:

• You dramatically increase the rate of transformation. In the past, we've seen 7 percent purchase conversion rates on magazine subscription renewals for B2C-sent emails, as opposed to the average 1 percent conversion rate with the traditional approach of gapped sentences.

• The quality of the mailing content gives the customer confidence in the company, which they are then more inclined to consider as a serious partner.

AI technologies used: ML, business rules engine, and NLG.
Configuration and setup time for an MVP: Plus or minus thirty-five human days.

Scenario 2: Personalized Online Customer Space

Let's say your website has a password-protected gated customer area. By accessing it, customers can track their current orders and access services reserved for existing customers. Typically, these pages include the contact information of the person who logs in, a table with up-to-date information related to the customer's account, graphics or photos of the products they have previously viewed on the site, and some general information. When sales information appears, it is a general marketing message addressed to all customers.

Description of the modern marketing solution: Thanks to AI, and reasoning based on the logged-in customer's known data, you can transform this customer area into an individualized sales platform. Potentially, anytime a customer looks for a product, you can explain online why this or that product is well adapted (or not) to their needs, based on an automatic study of their previous orders. The entire content of this customer area is generated on the fly according to each customer's unique context. The wow factor is guaranteed and the customer will come to rely on this free service, which becomes an ultra-personalized sales and loyalty marketing tool.

Gains obtained:

- You increase your sales without any additional sales cost.
- You improve customer retention because you offer a service ahead of the competition.

AI technologies used: Business rules engine, ML, and NLG.
Configuration and setup time for an MVP: approximately forty-five human days, but this figure may vary significantly depending on the scope of the range of services offered.

Scenario 3: Level 1 FAQs—Dynamic Frequently Asked Questions

Your products and services are marketed through multiple channels (direct sales force, distributors, telemarketing, internet, etc.). On your website, you have a FAQ page intended to answer customers' and prospects' most common questions. The content of each answer is generic, not personalized to the context of the customer and what they have just bought. This is why your customer service receives so many phone calls from customers who ask the same questions as those mentioned in the FAQ but who are looking for a personalized answer.

Description of the modern marketing solution: With an AI-based solution, you can invite the customer to connect to their personalized area with their password, where you can provide them with an individualized answer. By having them connect to your site, you can identify them via a cookie installed on their browser and base your reasoning on their actions on your website (downloads, products view, etc.). Which products did they just buy? Are they a VIP customer? Your answers can therefore be personalized according to this context. For example, if the customer has just purchased a type X heater, the answer will take into account this criterion and the list of FAQs will be considerably shortened because any irrelevant question will be excluded. In addition, the answers will include the name of the product purchased to motivate the customer to read the FAQ to the end: "For the type X heater that you bought on October 10, the warranty is valid for 12 months with factory return in the United States and Canada where you installed this product. To protect your investment, we suggest you add the North America Plus option to your maintenance contract. For only $250 pretax/year, you can benefit from on-site repair service." The dynamic FAQ can become an impressive marketing tool, as the best time to sell an additional service is when the customer is asking related questions and the company provides clear, reasoned answers, making it easy to purchase.

Gains obtained:

- You reduce the number of customer calls by 20 to 30 percent, but this is achieved over time as the deployment of dynamic FAQs takes place. The implementation can be done gradually, question by question, starting with the 20 percent of customer questions that generate 80 percent of the phone calls.
- You can sell upgrades and subscriptions, thus transforming the cost of customer service, often perceived as a cost center, into a profit center.
- For the customer, dynamic FAQs are a service that proves the seriousness of the supplier. It can thus become a factor in improving your image with your customers and drive website traffic based on organic sharing of the wow factor.

AI technologies used: Expert system, gapped sentences, or NLG.

Configuration and setup time: Twenty human days for setting up the application framework and the first question-and-answer set, then two to four human days per additional question and answer.

Scenario 4: Level 2 FAQs—Interactive Frequently Asked Questions

You have implemented the previous scenario and great results encourage you to go further!

Description of the modern marketing solution: Let's say you are an insurance agent and your customer asks if their medical insurance will cover an MRI and what the out-of-pocket cost would be. The answer would depend on the insurance level, what hospital the patient wants to use, and what agreements the company has with that hospital. In this instance, it's important to interact with the customer to understand if they were referred by their primary care physician, if they were referred by a hospital, if they have a choice of hospitals, and if there is an urgency in terms of timing. Of course, depending on the scenario, there could also be a series of questions driven by compliance or to mitigate legal risk.

As in the top-level FAQ, the second level requires the customer to log in to their personalized area with a password. But instead of writing all the answers to questions dynamically and on the fly, the company chooses, for some questions, to trigger a voice or written questionnaire to better understand the context. AI reasons on the customer's data, including details of their contract and the answers provided in the questionnaires, to offer an even more customized response.

Gains obtained:

- You can exceed the threshold of 50 percent of answers processed online rather than at your call center.
- Call center agents can then deal mainly with the more complex cases, the more interesting ones, with the help of collaborative AI.
- You collect additional data, such as information on how your customers use your products or services.
- You make the most of the communication, selling additional services.
- The same business rules knowledge base can be used by a cobot assisting call agents, who are themselves helping customers with the same questions.

AI technologies used: Rule and dialogue engine and NLU (if the questions prompt the customer to answer in an open way, such as to write an answer).

Configuration and setup time: Plus or minus ten human days per dialogue scenario, depending on the complexity of the topic.

Scenario 5: Product or Service Comparison

In a straightforward direct sales model, your salespeople try to steer the customer toward the right choice among a range of products. However, with the digitalization of online sales processes, the buyer can get information from social networks and via discussion forums and make their own choice without asking your team's opinion. You then run the risk that they might go to a competitor whose product might appear to be a better choice. Offering an online comparison solution is a new service that AI can do quite easily.

Description of the new service: On your website, the prospect clicks on the two products they want to compare. A dialogue engine opens to briefly ask them about the intended use. It then writes a personalized article with an argument that explains the difference with a use case example rather than just a table with two comparative columns of characteristics. In general, the application limits the customer to compare closed models. This approach is easier to set up.

Gains obtained:

• With a good argument, the system focuses on the added value in buying the premium model. But straight talk is important to build the trust that makes companies successful in the long run.

• Once again, you collect a large amount of usage data on what is important for your customers while respecting CCPA, GDPR or other data protection legislation.

AI technologies used: ML, expert system, NLU, and NLG.
Configuration and setup time: Fifty human days, but this figure may vary depending on the extent of the range of products or services.

Scenario 6: Automatic Advice for Selling Products or Services

Let's say you are an entrepreneur and you produce a range of electric bikes for different uses. Some are better suited for flat terrain, others for hilly routes, and so forth. You also offer different battery options, depending on the desired autonomy, as well as various accessories. You are trying to sell your quality product online, but prospects are confused by the number of factors to consider when searching for the bike that suits them best. How do they find the right bike? You set up a configurator, a user interface that helps put together the ideal bike, on your website, but sales results are disappointing. You then believe the only way to sell effectively is to talk to customers. You would need a team of good telemarketers, but this solution can be prohibitively expensive. Besides, you can't afford to start your own chain of stores or acquire a distributor network that would require huge margins and large capitalized inventories.

Analysis of the current situation: Like most traditional e-commerce sites, you display qualitative product photos and static description texts. The more the prospect tries to compare the products, the more questions they have, which delays them putting their selection in the cart. The FAQ page offers only general rules of use, such as if you climb hills regularly, you'll need a type XYZ battery and a more powerful engine. The answer is correct but is neither contextual nor sales oriented. It's not individualized expertise.

Description of the modern solution: With AI, you can allow prospects to describe their needs and the bicycle of their dreams in a free text field facilitated by a voice interface or a multiple-choice questionnaire. With a dialogue engine, you can confirm what the prospect is looking for by asking the right questions, just as your best in-store salesperson would, without any human interaction. The questions are short and smart, and each answer determines the next question. There is no decision tree. The expert system (using a deterministic approach) will find the best-suited electric bike along with useful options, even if the prospect does not tick all the boxes, and will write a business proposal automatically argued.

Gains obtained:

• The amount of collected data is of high quality because you collect not only basic information (first name, last name, address, etc.) but also prospects' use habits with the bike and otherwise. This enables you to define customer profiles and automate personalized follow-ups for each one of them.

• Such an approach to sales with individualized communication makes it possible to obtain conversion rates (visitors filling out a request or purchasing a bike) on an e-commerce site higher than 10 percent, although these conversions into purchases are not necessarily immediate.

• You only sell products that are in stock; therefore, your turnover rate is faster and you do not have to manage backorders.

• Customers seeking advice for a purchase are not the ones looking for the lowest price. They are more open to considering buying options that bring comfort and generate extra margin for you, the seller. By automating sales consulting, AI allows you to access the profile of customers with an above-average number of purchases on their track record.

• The quality of the reasoned sales proposal sent to the prospect develops their confidence in your company's brand, which helps justify a high price.

• If your sales model already includes a team of telemarketers, then with this new collaborative AI approach, the sales cycle is well on its way from the first telephone contact that follows the delivery of individualized sales advice.

AI technologies used: ML, expert system, NLU, and NLG.
Configuration and setup time: Plus or minus forty human days for an MVP, but this figure may vary depending on the extent of the range of products or services.

Here's an example of text that AI can write and then overlay on a video that shows the chosen product or display on the site in an answer window. If the customer leaves their contact information, the text can be the basis for a follow-up email. It reuses vocabulary used by the customer when defining their needs.

As you can see, the text produced is based on individualized expertise. Configurator rules are applied to the prospect's context in order to offer them advice in natural language on how to choose the bicycle that suits them best:

Dear Mrs. X,

We have analyzed your request to search for an electric bike for your daily commute to work. You mentioned that there is a fairly challenging hill along your route, that the daily distance is about twenty miles round trip, and that you must carry your computer on the bike in a secure way. You would also like to use the bike on weekends for trips of up to fifty miles, and you like the color white.

We suggest the AVELO-3400 model, which is available immediately. This bike is perfect for you because its battery is rather light, easy to remove for recharging at home, and therefore best adapted to your needs. The battery life we have chosen as an option covers approximately 120 miles, which means that you'd only have to recharge it once a week, and the engine is powerful enough to climb hills of medium difficulty. However, this model's screen does not include the Bluetooth connector you are requesting. What makes this bike one of a kind on the market is its shock absorber system, along with a most comfortable saddle that will make your daily commute very pleasant. Finally, we have added the padded and secure pannier that can hold both your computer bag and your purse. The bike, fully assembled with accessories, can be delivered to *your home within three days. The total cost comes to $1,490, all taxes included, which reflects our promotional discount valid only until the end of the week.*

Of course, this text may be longer or shorter depending on the context. The point here is to show that AI can write this type of text, allowing sales people to focus on sales negotiation, not on product evangelism.

Scenario 7: Customized Distribution Price

It is a complicated goal for the traditional retail sector to know which products interest each customer the most before they buy them. Yet it is an interesting basis for individualized tracking and customized offers—for example, by bundling two desired products for a promotional price. But how can you know a prospect's favorites when privacy laws limit the means of data collection without the store visitor's consent?

Description of the automation solution: With AI, and more specifically a machine learning approach, an American company has found a solution to this challenge: it encourages customers to use their smartphones to scan the labels of their favorite items to get a personalized price. This is always lower than the public price. It is truly a personalized discount, similar to the classic discount that a company gives to loyal customers. The factors that come into play in determining these discounted prices are known to avoid any perception of discrimination based on, for example, the client's age.

Loyalty via VIP Status

The technologies involved are based on approaches still unachievable only a few years ago. They rely on a large data set to model decisions based on dozens or even hundreds of dimensions. These systems provide in-depth knowledge not only of customer behavior but also of inventory, production capabilities, and even weather predictions. If, for example, bad weather is predicted midsummer in a seaside resort and some swimsuits are overstocked, this type of technology can determine what level of discount to offer to convince the soon-departing vacationer to purchase these swimsuits.

Gains obtained:

• The conversion rate with a personalized price is, of course, higher.

• The ratio of number of scans per article to immediate purchase rate is an important piece of information on prospects' perceived value of a product.

• The store becomes a data capture center by collecting valuable information on customer tastes with their consent.

• The solution makes it possible to negotiate lower prices with suppliers for customers who are trying their brand for the first time.

AI technologies used: ML.
Configuration and setup time: Plus or minus twenty to thirty human days for discovery and data analysis. Plus or minus forty to sixty human days for learning to set up ML.

AI's use cases for marketing are almost infinite. Customers no longer have time to read marketing materials and interpret generic answers for their context. They want truly individualized answers and content. They want to be treated as unique customers and to buy from known brands. They also want their sales contact people to offer them a range of products and services perfectly adapted to their needs. Collaborative AI will revolutionize the way companies and customers trade and should soon become the second language of marketers!

Five Areas of Collaborative AI Applications in the Services Sector

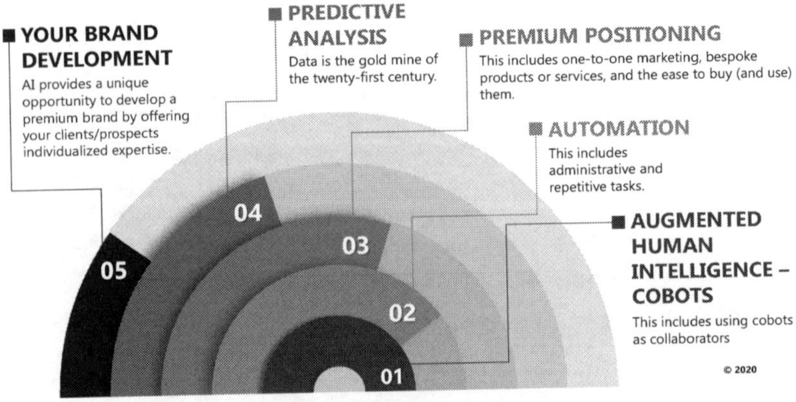

5.

How Will Collaborative AI Transform Your Work?

As more and more AI is entering into the world, more and more emotional intelligence must enter into leadership.

Amit Ray

The thought of robots replacing employees, and the potential consequences for labor in the future, is a frightening one. Images of fully robotized industrial assembly lines, regularly featured in the media, only reinforce this fear.

Yet technological reality proves that AI remains very far from matching the power of the human brain. According to some scientists, including Daphne Koller, a computer science professor at Stanford and founder of Coursera, the more progress made in technology, the farther we get from the idea of developing an AI that mimics the neurons of our brain.[22] This makes sense at a fundamental level. Apart from a sense of hubris, why would we build machines to look or operate like us? If you look at the robots deployed in manufacturing, it makes more sense to build robots to perfectly suit the use we have in mind for them. The idea of trying to mimic the human brain or the human form is interesting scientifically but makes little sense from a business perspective. We will explore this in greater detail when discussing the future of AI in the last chapter.

Even in industry, the goal of completely automating a process is no longer the priority. Preference is given to cobot-type machine tools that often produce much better results

---

22 *Martin Ford, Architects of Intelligence: The Truth about AI from the People Building It (Birmingham, UK: Packt, 2018).*

in terms of quality and efficiency. A factory worker is skilled at detecting defects early on and managing the unexpected, something that would not happen in a 100 percent automated factory. Moreover, many industrial robots are actually trained by highly skilled craftspeople, who then manage the robot to maintain quality.

At the same time, recent studies show levels of employee demotivation and labor productivity growth at near historic lows despite companies massively investing in the digitalization of information, its storage, and the deployment of new software applications. According to some human resources directors, knowledge workers mostly complain about being overwhelmed by work and having to perform repetitive and uninteresting tasks. Will AI, by automating repetitive tasks, change this trend and transform the nature of your professional activities?

This new work dimension in service activities, based on a clear division of labor between human and machine, will most likely have a major influence on the motivation, management style, and profiles of desirable candidates. What we do not know for sure is what percentage of work will go to technology and what will remain within the realm of employees. There are, however, many elements, as we mention next, that question the pessimistic predictions of AI's real effect on the workplace of the future and the future levels of human employment.

AI's Adoption Curve

If you look at the history of disruptive innovations and their adoption curves, you'll notice that it takes a lot more time for them to become mainstream than solution providers think. Why? Because beyond the technological advance, a breakthrough innovation disrupts work, purchasing and consuming habits, and sometimes even a population's culture. The imperfections of an innovative solution's early versions also slow down its adoption, especially when it involves automating an existing process.

The development of an innovation is a long process that is difficult to compress in time. Applying the Pareto principle of the 80/20 rule to this context shows that at first it is relatively easy to build a device that simulates 80 percent of a repetitive task, and efficiency gains are important during this first phase. However, even when this is feasible, the remaining 20 percent (the more complex elements) still represent 80 percent of the work to be done. This is what we see today with the success rates of deep learning.

In June 2018 in Beijing, AI won a competition against fifteen Chinese medical experts.[23] The AI solution took fifteen minutes to detect 87 percent of the brain tumors among 225 X-rays while the fifteen doctors took twice that amount of time and detected only 66 percent of them. Although AI was more successful than the doctors, these results still illustrate the reliability problem of some current AI technologies because AI missed 13 percent of the tumor cases. There is no realistic hope of arriving at a

23 *The BioMind AI software system used in this case was developed by the AI Research Centre for Neurological Disorders at Beijing Tiantan Hospital.*

100 percent reliable system with the current neural networks technology used for deep learning. It will take a new machine learning technology and perhaps a few decades to achieve a near-perfect result in a production context and thus reach the level of reliability that could eventually lead to fully replacing humans (the doctors in our example) with machines.

The delay for AI to become widely adopted for the complete automation of a company's activity will stretch out as long as humans continue to be intolerant of machine errors. For example, the self-driving car that killed a pedestrian in Arizona caused an immediate ban on testing for almost a year. Twenty-five years after the first successful trials (1994) of two Daimler car autopilots between Paris, France, and Lyon, France, the concept of a 100 percent autonomous car remains in the testing phase.[24] While in the summer of 2018 a tweet from Elon Musk announced the open source availability of his autopilot software, it also included a word of warning directed at the developer community, encouraging them to work on making the solution reliable. To illustrate this point, Luc Julia, VP at Samsung, said in November 2019 that fully autonomous cars [on the streets and for everybody] will never exist! Trying to reach perfection is a long-term proposition.

In the last chapter, we will discuss a new technological approach to self-learning that aims to meet the need for AI to produce reliable and understandable results. Each new technological move delays the adoption curve and therefore the moment when AI might become a threat to employment. This is

24 *"The Prometheus Project Launched in 1986: Pioneering Autonomous Driving," Daimler, accessed October 15, 2019, https://media.daimler.com/marsMediaSite/en/instance/ko/The-PROMETHEUS-project-launched-in-1986-Pioneering-autonomous-driving.xhtml?oid=13744534.*

why AI's scope until at least 2050 will be based primarily on a human-machine collaboration rather than on a 100 percent automation of human work.

AI's Limitations

What AI can and cannot do fundamentally determines how much AI can transform our work and its future organization. We read so many articles that recount AI's many feats that it seems appropriate, in this chapter, to address its limits today: AI has no common sense, no real creativity, no empathy, and no real sense of humor! Above all, it has no consciousness, a term that we do not really know how to define in the context of a robot. AI has no self-awareness, and the more you learn how AI systems are programmed, the more you realize that AI is less magic and more impressive computational programming.

AI and Common Sense

Common sense is based on a mix of knowledge and culture. It therefore requires general intelligence that involves value judgment and multidisciplinary experience, which the simple AI available today does not possess. The AI algorithm that won the Go game against the best player in the world does not know how to play chess or poker. It is therefore monodisciplinary and can rely only on the knowledge of the Go game to develop a form of common sense. If common sense is necessary in general decision-making (as opposed to a vertical and specific decision), people will remain essential for a long time to come.

AI and Creativity

We've all heard from various media that AI can create paintings, music, and cooking recipes. However, in these examples, AI is used to detect patterns—for example, to determine musical rhythms, colors, and tastes—that end users like in order to synthesize the successful ingredients and "create" a new piece of music, a new canvas, or a new recipe. But these are just analyses, syntheses, and copies of preexisting styles. They do not involve creative imagination.

One of the most interesting AI research avenues is creative AI.[25] The company DeepMind, a subsidiary of Google, shows impressive videos where AI finds solutions by itself to win video games.[26] This example proves that significant progress is being made and that AI can learn from its mistakes and its successes to achieve specific goals. Nonetheless, the goal and the definition of a victory are relatively simple in a game. In addition, AI performs real-time analyses of previous game rounds to determine what works and what doesn't work toward achieving any specific goal, drawing conclusions from this to make forward progress. This is not creativity in the true sense of the term. In business, the amount of nonobjective or long-term metrics makes an end goal much more complex and far beyond what AI can "invent." Still, an analysis of what works and what doesn't can become an interesting avenue for knowledge workers to explore.

---

25 *Experiments with Google offers examples of how researchers are adopting AI to attempt creative projects. The website is updated from time to time and worth following: https://experiments.withgoogle.com.*

26 *See the DeepMind website at https://deepmind.com.*

Creativity is a human psychological process that aims to imagine a concept, an object, or a solution with a new proposition. We stand at the opposite end of what conventional computers can do, which is having a rational approach based on the analysis of existing data. In business, creativity includes managing the unexpected as well and therefore remains the prerogative of knowledge workers today.

A prime example is contingency management, which is integral in our professional lives. It can be included here because it requires creativity to imagine the possible scenarios and how we might address them.

AI and Empathy

Empathy is defined by the ability to feel emotions experienced by others. AI does not feel. Some AI solution providers are developing robots able to analyze human faces or written exchanges in electronic format to detect emotions. The software is based on so-called sentiment analysis technologies. These applications are certainly interesting but cannot be described at this point as showing any real empathy, since that requires a conscience and an understanding of others' feelings.

AI and Humor

Humor is a real roadblock for AI and more specifically for NLU. It is a means of expression where we sometimes say the opposite of what we mean to get a reaction, or we allude to a context without expressing it clearly. Humor is affected by culture, and each culture has its own humor codes. This leaves the computer's "neurons" in the dust. Understanding a humorous text will remain the prerogative of human beings for the near future.

Thus, AI is still different from human intelligence in many areas. Any task that requires common sense, creativity, empathy, or humor won't be able to be automated by AI for a very long time, not until the arrival of AGI, likely at the end of the century. We will discuss this in the last chapter. As applied research progresses, AI will focus on complementarity with humans because the machine simply cannot replace them.

Collaborative AI Influences Motivation

Past experience deploying small and ambitious AI projects has shown that AI-based solutions are well perceived by knowledge workers when the approach is correctly explained to them and the tool is used to improve employee efficiency. This change brings about a new level of motivation that can fuel the company's success. Knowledge workers keep using their creativity and common sense to improve business processes while also conscientiously monitoring the machine so that it doesn't automate any errors.

We recently worked with an organization where a few hundred employees were doing the same consulting work for about one million customers. We followed their development of a cobot to help knowledge workers—a cobot intended not only to help a consultant understand a client's exact situation in mere seconds but also to ask them the right questions and offer personalized recommendations in return. In a nutshell, the cobot's goal was to promote intelligent discussion in addition to using the existing CRM. After the prototype was deployed for a few months in a test agency, the site manager summed up the added value provided by AI to his context in these five points:

1. Customers have more respect for a knowledge worker (using a cobot) because they can immediately see how competent they are, as they do not ask random questions and get straight to the point.
2. For the employee, the discussion atmosphere is less tense because their customers know they bring them added value in the form of reasoned advice (suggested by AI) that analyzes their situation, compares it to others, and recommends relevant areas to pursue.
3. For the adviser, the work is less stressful because it is focused on the customer relationship rather than on the relevance of what they say, and they are not afraid of forgetting important points that could be held against them later in case of a mistake.
4. The administrative work of reporting which actions were agreed upon between the employee and their client, as well as any follow-up, is automated. The work done by the machine is of remarkable quality and eliminates tedious tasks.
5. The knowledge worker is free of any constraints. AI does not decide; it only suggests. Just like a GPS suggests were we should go.

In general, the company will have to rely on motivated employees to suggest AI-automated business process improvements, thanks to their common sense and creativity. This requirement is more complex in service activities than in industry. Always keeping an ear to the ground, sharing information, and giving thanks and respect where they are due—all this will help achieve this goal. We must build a working atmosphere where most employees understand the added value they bring to the company in order to develop their creativity.

An employee's motivation also guarantees their professional conscience. The worst scenario, in any business, is to automate an incorrect process. The error may then be repeated thousands of times without any employee reacting.

AI must be set up not only with the goal of being accepted by knowledge workers but also with the goal of becoming friendly and smart enough so that the knowledge workers themselves want to become part of the collaborative AI project to make it even better.

Collaborative AI Influences the Quality of Work

Initially, simple AI will help the knowledge worker perform tasks that are difficult to complete due to lack of time. How many salespeople in your company prepare for their appointment with an existing customer by integrating all available data about them in the CRM, reviewing each catalog offer to select the most relevant ones, and gathering all the questions in writing so that the meeting is as fruitful as possible? How many maintenance technicians are perfectly familiar with all the appliance models their employer asks them to troubleshoot and know how to properly question their clients in order to reach a relevant diagnosis? Probably not many. In service activities, work is often done in a traditional way. A solution is tried to see if it works, and too bad if three spare parts are unnecessarily replaced instead of just one.

Collaborative AI, by supporting employees and increasing rigorous implementation on their part, will automate this type of activity and lower operational costs related to errors. This new AI approach will therefore increase the quality of the work accomplished.

This trend in services automation will also change the profile of employees that companies recruit because the sought-after qualities will gradually evolve.

Collaborative AI Influences the Qualities Required of Employees

To illustrate our point, let's go back to the profile of sales and marketing employees as it concerns all companies. Today, recruiting a top-notch sales force is more often than not asking for the impossible. The sales manager is looking for salespeople able to understand the full catalog of products or services sold by the company, often an increasingly sophisticated one, in order to set themselves apart from the competition. For this, they seek to recruit people with professional experience in their sector who often have worked for the competition. The sales manager also wants the sales force to be real salespeople with highly developed relational and even emotional intelligence. In other words, the manager is looking for salespeople with broad analytical skills; knowledge of the products, services, and markets; the ability to analyze and synthesize existing customer data; the capacity to quickly learn any new best practices; and the intelligence to understand new products or services, all with a perfect command of existing regulations as well as a developed relational intelligence. This type of profile is rare, to say the least. The high-performing analytical employee is not necessarily the best in client relationships. With simple AI, the customer data analysis, determination of the best possible offer, and compliance management are all entrusted to the machine. The salesperson focuses on their customer relationships with a limited risk of a consulting error because they have the AI system to help them.

The ideal profile sought for your sales force is easier to define. It describes an excellent salesperson with good interpersonal skills when dealing with customers. Their experience in your particular sector is of less importance, since AI-based cobots will help them build specific business skills very quickly, but this outside experience can augment them in their daily activity.

This shows that in the medium term, professional experience, often partial as it is, will tend to lose some value on the labor market for line positions (as opposed to those requiring expertise) and that relational intelligence will become an essential quality, both externally in customer relationships and internally in employee and colleague relationships.

There is a common case, often referred to, where a call center has reduced the field training time for telemarketers from six months to fifteen days thanks to AI. Traditionally, training a call center customer support agent in the telecommunication sector takes about six months, which is a major challenge because staff turnover rates in call centers are notoriously high. But with AI, more specifically a cobot, the call center reduced the training to fifteen days because candidates no longer needed a lot of experience to be successful. This type of job will be accessible to all those with the right qualities—namely, strong interpersonal skills to welcome customers over the phone (relational intelligence)—and candidates may or may not need any specific telecommunication experience. Empathy, patience, and clarity of expression will become more important than the five years spent working for a competitor. For the majority of job openings, self-management skills will become a more important qualification than know-how and experience. Many of us will be able to become experienced in a field without going back to school simply by practicing with the help of a cobot specialized in a specific trade. AI may be a great opportunity for those who find themselves marginalized in our society due to a lack of specialization because the power of collaborative AI, notably a cobot, is that it trains and upskills the workforce.

Here's an anecdote to illustrate this point: Up until a few years ago, taxi drivers from European countries went to a taxi school for months, where they learned to memorize thousands of city streets. Today, GPS has voided this requirement because it determines the best route with much more relevance than an experienced taxi driver, taking into account real-time traffic data. Customers no longer rate a taxi driver based on their ability to drive them quickly from one point to another, but rather they appreciate and value a driver's friendliness, the cleanliness of their vehicle, and their ability to adapt their driving to traffic conditions. Self-management skills become more important than the years of experience driving in a perfectly mapped-out city. By changing the nature of a job, collaborative AI—and in this context, cobots—will promote hiring based on different sorts of candidate profiles.

Another change that AI could affect in employee recruiting is linked to two qualities often perceived as opposites: creativity and discipline. Nowadays, given the rather traditional nature (in the noble sense of the term) of many tasks performed in the service sector, managers in charge of developing their teams are looking for potential employees who are organized and able to replicate their service production process in a rigorous way. The advantage is often given to the industry-minded candidate over the creative type who seeks to innovate. But AI will change this trend and creativity will regain great value in companies. Creative AI is in its infancy and, for now, works only when the stated goal is a simple one, which is not the case in business, where the goals are varied and sometimes contradictory (for instance, the simultaneous objectives of strong growth and profitability in a company). Employee creativity will become key to improving existing processes while today, in most cases, emphasis is put on simplicity of execution for both speed and a reduced risk of errors. For example, a lawyer tends to use a contract template rather than starting from scratch. With AI and its future derived applications, the emphasis will be put on accuracy with automatic custom-made contract drafting, instantly executed by a machine. Creativity will claim a greater place as we evolve toward a world that produces mostly bespoke offerings in an industrial way and fewer and fewer off-the-shelf options.

Professions that require great creativity, such as designers or those who create new services or improve processes, will remain in the realm of human workers, and their value on the job market will increase.

Collaborative AI Influences the Organization of Work Augmented by Cobots

In a service company, management will face several challenges and opportunities in the implementation of collaborative AI. Artificial intelligence will bring a competitive advantage to their core business (both the quality of services provided and the ability to offer new ones), and pioneers will become the market leaders. Management will have to recruit the best business experts in their field to provide the highest performing collaborative platform in their activity sector. We will therefore see four main profiles in a company:

1. Augmented workers: Employees who work with a cobot. The recruitment criteria will be mainly self-management skills and relational intelligence. The nature of

their work will change, as previously mentioned in chapter 3 in the section on Employees Augmented and Freed by Cobots.

2. Expert employees: These workers take care of the tasks that cobots can't perform. Experts will be a level above augmented workers, able to address problems that a cobot can't, but these experts are not likely to update the cobot itself.

3. Citizen developers: These employees will be in a position to improve cobots' business rules to make them more efficient and able to manage more and more situations.

4. Managers: Employees who recruit and motivate their teams. They will not be business experts but rather generalists in charge of recruiting and keeping their teams productive.

In certain specific areas of activity, this model will probably have to be adapted, but the goal here is to draw your attention to the human influence of AI, which can change your business model and thus internal organization while creating great development and growth opportunities for all employees.

Collaborative AI Influences Training

In the future, company training will focus primarily on the general culture of the activity sector but also on employee self-management skills and motivation while cobots will train knowledge workers in their daily tasks.

AI will also affect teaching methods. Basic training has seen few changes since the emergence of printing in the fifteenth century. It is still based on books and class notes. One reason for the relative failure of traditional school systems, where one teacher oversees a few dozen students, is the inability of the teacher to adapt their method to each individual student. For example, there are many different ways to understand history—memorizing dates and names is just one approach. What is true for schools also applies to continuing education in companies.

Course videos are getting better, and massive open online courses are a real breakthrough, but they mainly involve onscreen course visualization, rather than a paper medium, with a multiple-choice questionnaire validation that is not very demanding of the student. We can logically predict that the training revolution will be based on the gamification of learning, or a format similar to the most sophisticated video games, but with these additional elements:

- Software that tests each student to understand how they learn each subject. Adapting to each student's learning style and capabilities is the best way to avoid failure, and this can be achieved with AI.
- The serious game must above all be fun and motivating to keep the student's interest. In this time of social networks, catching anyone's attention for more than a few minutes is a real challenge. Serious games based on AI should be able to extend attention spans.
- The solutions will generate customized exercises, explain the reason for each error in natural language through a dialogue

with the student, and automatically regenerate a new exercise to validate the acquired knowledge. The student will make progress following a training path where the obstacles to be overcome are the exercises to solve.

We should witness a real revolution in this area. In this scheme, the role of teachers and trainers will evolve toward one of psychological support and personalized counseling. Teachers will also help students develop their creativity, curiosity, and practical work: they will be able to develop their own applications on a serious game platform for specific use cases. Joël de Rosnay, the famous scientist and former research associate at Massachusetts Institute of Technology, is very much involved in the future vision of AI. He even claims that the length of doctors' studies could be shortened. They will no longer be asked primarily for knowledge but rather to connect the relevant information, since the machine will prepare the appointment between the patient and the doctor and help the doctor make the correct diagnosis.

Overall, experience working in collaboration with cobots will become an essential qualification that will stand out on any candidate's résumé, just as the use of the Microsoft Office Suite and basic computing do now. So, too, will the common sense necessary to understand tasks that AI-based cobots can or cannot do become essential. In the future, any choice of training will have to be made keeping this criterion in mind.

Collaborative AI Influences Decision-Making

The question of whether AI will make decisions by itself on complex subjects is a topic of discussion that often surfaces in professional circles. Even if we exclude fully automated processes, such as simple reasoning on large volumes of data, it is likely that businesses and knowledge workers are working toward that goal. This approach will be possible only when the decisions to be made do not involve any risk and do not require any value judgment, creativity, or common sense. In many cases, AI will suggest a choice of decisions that need to be validated by humans. The main objective of collaborative AI will be the reliability and traceability of the service provided (for example, the quality of the advice provided to customers), not the replacement of employees. Also, demand for personalized services will increase and thus require more and more augmented workers.

As previously mentioned, it is likely that the productivity gains linked to the deployment of cobots will not come from automatic decision-making but rather from improved reliability of answers and relevance of solutions recommended by knowledge workers equipped with this AI-based virtual assistant. Thanks to cobots, time will no longer be wasted on errors, a bit like a GPS saving precious minutes each day by choosing the best route, offering alternative choices but not replacing the driver and their ability to choose another route. Cobots are here to stay, and thousands of companies around the world are developing them every day. The technologies to implement them are available today, helping to improve decision-making and employee well-being, as the use of these tools reduces their work-related stress. AI therefore allows these workers to devote themselves entirely to what they know how to do best—namely, to make strategic decisions.

We firmly believe that the next decades will be years of human-machine collaboration rather than those of human competing with machine. We believe that together, human and machine can accomplish more than they could individually. Most employees will enjoy working with collaborative AI that augments them because it will mean less stress, more accurate and personalized answers in seconds, and completely automated repetitive work. Humans, with our common sense, ability to judge, creativity, and professional conscience, can be fully focused on validating the quality of service and advice produced by AI. Regardless of this progress, the superiority of the human mind will remain indispensable to accomplish quality tasks and will continue to fascinate researchers with its complexity and elusiveness. While collaborative AI will become increasingly important in society, from an economic point of view, the relevant question will not be how much work remains for knowledge workers but rather how to share the wealth that automation generates.

Finally, let's keep in mind that any new technology can be used in a positive or a negative way. For instance, nuclear physics is the basis of MRI, an indispensable modern medical marvel, but it is also used to make bombs that kill on a massive scale. This dichotomy is also true for AI. But buying into merchants of fear speeches that demonize AI, just as they did the printing press in the Middle Ages, will not help clarify how AI can serve humankind. Our goal here is to objectively analyze AI's effect on the labor market today and tomorrow.

6.

Seven Keys to a Successful First AI Project

If we don't know how machines make decisions, we shouldn't trust them to determine our fates.

Greg Satell[27]

27 *Greg Satell and Josh Sutton, "We Need AI That Is Explainable, Auditable, and Transparent," Harvard Business Review, October 28, 2019, https://hbr.org/2019/10/we-need-ai-that-is-explainable-auditable-and-transparent.*

We have deployed or supervised dozens of AI projects in the United States, Europe, and Asia-Pacific regions. This experience has led us to pinpoint mistakes to avoid and best practices to follow, which in turn yielded a list of key tips for a successful first AI project. To fully understand our proposed approach, we must specify that the first objective of AI is usually not reducing direct costs. This statement was also true of the factory robotization that took place in the second half of the twentieth century. The return on investment was eventually most often realized but only after five to ten years. Automation was deployed primarily to increase the quality, reliability, and traceability of manufactured goods.

The ultimate goal of producing bespoke products at off-the-shelf prices using digital machines has been difficult to achieve in the past and remains so today. The best example of the success of automated manufacturing comes from Toyota. In the early 1980s, Toyota was a fairly small regional player with some presence in the Western markets. When Toyota embraced automation, it did so with several goals in mind—to scale its offer, improve quality, offer new features, and cut costs. Toyota used technology to scale its processes, grow its margins, and expand the company. Today, Toyota describes this strategy as a human-powered-automation move, and it is this successful approach that has led to competing with Volkswagen and Renault-Nissan for the world's number-one automaker.[28]

To paraphrase Toyota, human-powered AI is the winning approach to adopt when talking about AI projects in service activities. The goal is to opt for technical progress in offering new services with high added value while ensuring that knowledge workers do not feel threatened by AI. With this in mind, let's now discuss which questions to ask at the start of an initiative, how to organize the project to serve the stakeholders, and what type of internal communication to promote.

Seven Keys to a Successful First AI Project

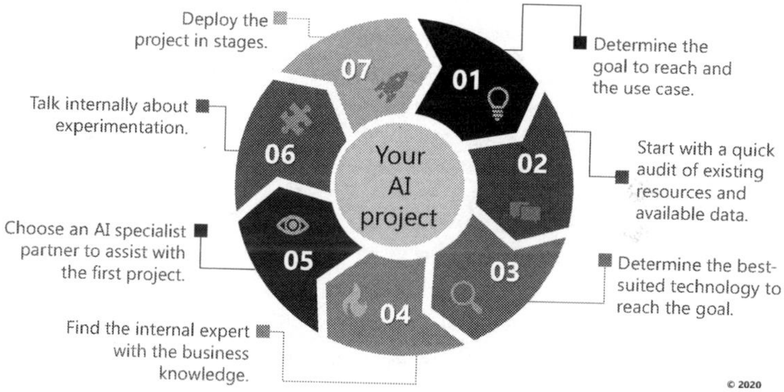

Launching a first project based on collaborative AI is a strategic choice. You must first reflect on your company's business model and what you want to achieve. How do you use AI to transform your catalog so that your services are not only easy to sell but

28 *Jeff Rothfeder, "At Toyota, the Automation Is Human-Powered," Fast Company, September 5, 2017, http://www.fastcompany.com/40461624/how-toyota-is-putting-humans-first-in-an-era-of-increasing-automation.*

also become especially easy to buy? Which unique services should you offer to appeal to your and your competitors' customers? Sometimes this involves an approach you could not have previously imagined because the automation of individualized expertise was not possible before AI.

In the service sector, the core business is essentially based on the use of gray matter. This can be expensive. As a result, many services that clients expect (if only rarely) are clearly not available. The ratio of price to value-added of these services is too high using the available traditional technology to democratize them. AI, by automating individualized expertise, paves the way for the improvement or creation of thousands of new services that will generate additional sales revenue and enable innovative companies to push their competitors aside to become the leaders of tomorrow. Collaborative AI not only changes the way you communicate and negotiate with your customers (in particular by using cobots that make interaction between them and knowledge workers much richer and more constructive) but also how your collaborators work, sharing their tasks with cobots.

It is this line of strategic thinking that you must use to determine the company's most appropriate use case that will serve to launch a first project. Here are the three questions you should ask yourself to identify your first AI project:

1. Business model: What are your customers and prospects waiting for? More specifically, which client frustrations would you like the new AI-based service to solve? If your business model does not solve a pressing need for your customers, it is at risk.

2. Business plan: Which services in your business could be fundamentally improved by AI and allow you to increase your price list? Which new services could you produce through automated individualized expertise to meet your customers' needs? Delivering these would set you apart from your competitors in a significant way or make your services more obvious and simpler to buy or use.

3. ROI: What approximate price would your customers eventually be willing to pay for the new service(s)? Or, if this new service can collect usage data on your customers and prospects, how much financial value would you attribute to each set of data acquired? The ROI is often difficult to estimate before the solution is put into production, but the definition of your ROI assumptions remains a decisive element in judging the relevance of the project over the long term and for evaluating a project in hindsight.

Start with an Audit of the Present Situation

Once the project based on the use case is identified, it's time to study its technical feasibility. As previously mentioned, the quality of data is critical in the majority of AI projects. It is therefore important for companies that want to move forward to determine what data already exists in the company, how it is collected (manually or automatically by connected objects, for instance), and if it is centralized in a company's shared database. If not, how can it be accessed; if so, in what format is it available? Either way, how can it be ethically and legally collected?

An audit of a current situation goes beyond data. It usually takes a few days to answer the following questions:

- Present situation: Which business areas are covered by existing IT, and how will the collaborative AI project add value to existing processes, productivity, and customer services?
- Feasibility: What data should be used, how should it be obtained, and with which tool(s)? What is the technical foundation in place, and which AI technologies and user interfaces are of interest?
- Relevance: What is the match between intent and available resources for the project?
  - Intent: What are the current IT projects, how are they adapted to the various needs and objectives of each service, and how can the chosen AI project optimize them?
  - Resources: What internal effort (availability, computer scientists' workloads, etc.) and what development and maintenance budgets are planned?

It is only after this stage that you'll be able to determine the cost of the project and what the company's first step toward AI should be.

Experience has shown that it is preferable for the data needed for an AI project to be assessed by an external stakeholder rather than by someone internal to the company.

Determine the Best Technologies for a Project

Even if it is up to an IT architect to choose the best components, it is interesting to review the questions that must be asked. As you have seen in the projects that we have discussed, collaborative AI projects often require the use of several different AI technologies, so working with a consultancy that specializes in AI may make the most sense for you. If your project involves purchasing a packaged solution (for example, one that covers image, sound, or text recognition), it is the software package publisher who should determine which platform or AI software is best suited for you. However, if your project refers to a management topic that touches your core business and you are looking for a custom-made solution that integrates your best practices and stands out from your competition, then it's important to consider these non-exhaustive questions:

- Must the expected results from the application be completely accurate, or is a margin of error acceptable? For example, if the application is to suggest which type of tools to acquire in order to solve a specific technical problem, personalized advice produced by an AI-based application must be accurate. On the other hand, if you are just looking for prospects to buy product X next week, then less accurate advice is acceptable. In the first case, you would choose among deterministic technologies with reasoning that is based on precise but modifiable rules. In the second, the statistical approach is allowable. The next chapter will give you more details on these available technologies.

- For human language comprehension, does your application have to understand the client's voice or a written question? Should you immediately understand the meaning of what is said or written by the user? Can you reverse the process by asking the computer to ask close-ended questions?
- Regarding language generation aspects, what type of text do you need to receive? Comments? Situation summaries? Diagnostics? Reasoned recommendations? Is the application supposed to work as a black box and make decisions itself, or must a knowledge worker intervene to validate the final answer or to make intermediate choices? For example, for mass sales canvassing (hundreds to thousands of prospects) to sell low-value products, you might allow the application to write and send emails to potential customers without a human reviewing them first. If, however, you are targeting major account prospects or VIP customers, it is probably better for an operator to validate or even enrich the messages sent by following such rules as *all quotes over $XK...*or *all prospects making more than $XM in sales revenue...*

Of course, these questions address only two areas of AI: reasoning (including self-learning) and language processing. Other areas may also be considered, depending on the project. Nonetheless, in service activities, the core business is commonly structured around those two areas.

Find an Expert Internally

A collaborative AI project is not a project that is outsourced to the IT department from the outset. This type of project is much too important to a company's core business to be managed by only a technical team. AI projects require visionaries who understand the company's market positioning, its current customers, and above all, what strategic direction it wants to follow. The first project is likely to be the automation of new services that can induce change to the business model in the medium term. Alternatively, it may be directed toward assisting employees overwhelmed by repetitive tasks that they perceive to be useless. General management must get involved because the effect of a collaborative AI project will be structural.

The ideal team is driven by a business expert who understands the frustration each end customer feels in searching for a unique answer, which the AI-based final application will address. The right expert is the one most experienced in the line of business involved in the project, who knows all the unwritten facts about it within the company. It is not the one who focuses on the aesthetics of the final solution but indeed the one who best understands the customers, their possible frustrations, and what they are searching for, sometimes without them ever clearly expressing themselves. This person will keep the entire project team focused on one specific goal: to provide appropriate answers that delight and surprise customers while making competitors tremble. This expert will be a conductor who surrounds themselves with a diverse band.

The team in charge of setting up the project technically must include people with multidisciplinary skills, such as an engineer with computer science and IT skills. It will surely include a developer who will focus on data preparation, and a systems architect who will select the most appropriate technologies for the project (these last two functions may be outsourced, as mentioned in the previous paragraph).

The expert and the business participants will define the *why* and the *what to do*, and the computer scientist will work on the *how to do it* aspects of the project. Success will come from their ability to understand one another and to work together, so, as always, picking the right team is critical.

Choose an AI Specialist Partner

Too many IT projects fail because everything was done internally. The new-generation AI brings something new. In light of its success, the available supply of AI tools is extensive and renews every year, so you have many options. Trying to choose the right platform (remotely hosted software) internally doubles the risk of failure. As mentioned before, many AI projects also require several different AI technologies, so it makes sense to consider AI agencies that are focused on bringing their customers the best of AI technology. Here are some simple and common-sense criteria that can help you make the right choice when selecting an external service provider:

- Avoid AI fanatics—those who think that all problems can be solved with AI and that robots will run the world from 2025 onward. Reasonable experts know that it takes more time than this for a technology to mature and be adopted.

- Make sure that their definition of *AI* is not limited to machine learning or deep learning (self-learning). This is all too common. As stated at the beginning of the book, the definition of *AI* established in 1956 suggested a much wider scope. Self-learning is an important pillar of AI but not the only one, especially in services, where the core business relies on deterministic reasoning and communication among humans.
- Make sure their technology will easily work with other conventional and AI technology. Too often AI companies think that customers only need their technology and don't even think about how their technology might or might not work with existing infrastructure.
- And, of course, do speak with customers who have been helped by AI specialists to understand the nature of their experiences and the added value brought to their projects.

Several duties can be assigned to an external service provider. These are the three most important ones to consider:

1. Choosing the best available technology and platform to meet your expressed needs. A computer architect often fills this role.
2. Analyzing the data available or the data to be collected. The more accurate and diverse data your company collects, the more value your AI applications will generate.

3. Offering an outside perspective that yields strategic advice. Working with your company, the external service provider will need to be able to define and record your customers' unexpressed needs.

Experiment and Communicate Internally

In the current context where discussing AI conjures up risks for employment, it is important, internally, to state from the start what boundaries are planned for the first application of collaborative AI. You will have to reassure your employees on two points:

1. This project is not intended to replace anyone in the company. The goal is to create new services—for example, to develop a cobot that will help a group of employees overwhelmed by administrative tasks. As previously mentioned, no AI can completely replace a company function. Therefore, for the next decades, AI will be applied only to specific tasks and you will create collaborative tools for your employees. Without their committed involvement in this project, the company will not meet the anticipated success.

2. The expected positive results will not necessarily be seen right away. It is therefore important, internally, to discuss experimenting and giving this idea a chance, as its implementation will most likely require constant fine-tuning over the first few months. When you are the first in your

sector to deploy a new idea, you must be both humble and resilient. Don't throw the baby out with the bathwater after an initial partial success.

It is for these two reasons that the project manager must be a good and strong communicator.

Deploy the Project Step-by-Step

A collaborative AI project is always deployed incrementally, if possible, in monthly intervals. The first iteration that can really be tested is referred to as the MVP. This is followed by incremental improvements over the next phases based on user feedback. Projects that run for too long on new technologies often end up off topic by the time of delivery.

As with any typical project, each new iteration has three phases:

1. Defining the goal
2. Preparing the data and development of the application or algorithm
3. Implementing and testing in real life

With these points in mind, you are well on your way to launching your first AI project. In the next chapter, we will discuss the available technologies to do so.

7.

Taking the Technology Further

More pathetic than the digital age is the people who love it. They buy right into the "newer is always better" ideology.

Rebecca McNutt[29]

29 *Rebecca McNutt is a futurist and the author of Bittersweet Symphony (Seattle: Amazon Digital Services, 2017).*

This chapter addresses the technological dimension of AI. It is purposely near the end of the book because the goal here is not to talk about AI technology but about the business potential of collaborative AI for your business. However, some general technological knowledge on this subject is necessary in order to understand the possibilities and the limits of available technologies.

AI is a broad term that encompasses a large number of technologies and tools assembled to offer business solutions that are complementary to human intelligence. There are seven broad categories of tools, technologies, or methods that can be used at different stages of a collaborative AI project:

1. Data preparation tools
2. Available technologies for machine learning
3. Available solutions for reasoning on data without self-learning
4. Updates on visual recognition
5. State-of-the-art methods in text and voice recognition
6. Tools for generating texts or voices
7. The right approach to automate decision-making

These seven technological approaches all correspond to one type of artificial intelligence, simple AI, the only category of AI that is in production in companies today. These are also the options that enable you to set up collaborative AI solutions for your business. We won't name specific tools because the available options evolve too quickly, and this book is not intended to be a guide to AI technologies. Although AGI (multidisciplinary) and super artificial intelligence as portrayed in science fiction films do not exist, we will talk about these possibilities in the next chapter. For now, let's discuss simple AI and the broad categories of an AI project.

Data Preparation

Data is the keystone of AI. First, the available data must be of good quality (unique and not redundant), understandable by computer software (thus generally structured), and correct (avoiding obsolescence and with strong internal data governance procedures in place that are being followed). The second key factor, especially with deep learning, which we will discuss later, is the availability of large volumes of data. The accuracy and relevance of resulting machine learning algorithms depend on large volumes of data. Finally, the diversity of data is the third essential quality factor for an AI project. If the self-learning algorithm is trained on data not representative of a population, it will, unsurprisingly, generate an incoherent or illogical program outcome. To put it another way, you need large amounts of representative data that includes all the different scenarios you might want the algorithm to deal with. This issue is solved with data preparation or data-wrangling tools.

The goal of this new generation of tools, which appeared in the early 2010s, in particular Dataiku, Alteryx, or Trifacta, is to allow business users to easily link together several data sources of different natures. In addition, these tools include modules that make it easy to control data quality, such as preventing a male patient from being marked pregnant in a medical file, which would be nonsense in the physical world but a common type of error in databases.

Thanks to data wrangling, the data assembly and refinement steps on which algorithms train have improved from a long and very technical process (with extract, transform, load-type software) to one accessible to business users. In other words, they are now accessible to any employee with the level of computer training required to create Excel charts with a few somewhat complex formulas. That's good news!

Data outlines the history of the company. If it is of good quality, why not use it to create custom programs or algorithms from a defined business goal? This is the purpose of self-learning systems.

Machine Learning from Data

It is the dream of computer science's founding fathers to create software that writes computer programs without any human intervention. In the AI context, it is a matter of creating a machine that does the following:

- Learn beyond the limits of a human brain's capacity (one hundred terabytes of memory maximum) or those of reasoning (Miller's law).

- Automatically generate algorithms able to solve complex tasks and take into account thousands of special cases. This functionality would occur against the backdrop of the somewhat simplistic idea that if AI could learn without limits, then it could grow more intelligent than humans.

There are two main methods of software learning: the statistical approach and the rule procedure. The statistical approach is most often based on an artificial neural network technology. This is a network of interconnected nodes that more or less mimic the neural connections of the human brain. Although not new, this technology has grown considerably since the 2010s thanks to the explosion of available data and the constant improvement of its performance.

Artificial neural networks can take on many forms and many different learning methods. They are generically referred to as machine learning. This is a broad area and going into much detail here would be off topic. Nevertheless, the term *deep learning* is frequently encountered in the press and deserves attention. Deep learning provides a smart learning method that manipulates synapses layer by layer for greater accuracy. Deep learning is not limited to a numerical result, such as a score or a classification. It can also be used to automatically subtitle photos. As with any statistical method, deep learning requires large volumes of data to work properly.

The goal of deep learning is to learn automatically, especially from unstructured (informal) data analysis. As of 2019, it remains the only technology that gives significant results on sound, image, or video data processing. Google uses it to find street numbers from images saved for Google Maps.[30] Deep learning is also at the heart of diagnostics in medical radiology. Specifically, the software has been harnessed to analyze medical images (X-rays, MRIs, etc.) to look for tumors and other abnormalities.[31] This approach to AI may be especially suitable for large companies, but at any scale, it is important to keep an eye on this technology despite the defects that limit its scope.

Currently, artificial neural networks present certain drawbacks, as briefly mentioned in the first chapter. Let's discuss these in further detail.

One drawback is that although input data does not need to be structured initially, it does need to be formalized into a series of decimals corresponding to the weighting of the input neurons. While this allows all data to be processed, since data can always be transformed into a series of decimals, it can be a considerable handicap when it comes to processing more formal data, such as text. A data pretreatment method is necessary to get this formalization.

Artificial neural networks also require a data training period that can last between a few hours and a few weeks. Recurrent artificial neural networks are even more prone to this downside.

To obtain meaningful results, the machine must be trained with large volumes of data that cover all the special cases. This therefore significantly extends the training period. Combined

30 *"Updating Google Maps with Deep Learning and Street View," Google AI Blog, May 3, 2017, https://ai.googleblog.com/2017/05/updating-google-maps-with-deep-learning.html.*

31 *Andrew Wade, "How AI Is Powering a Revolution in Medical Diagnostics," The Engineer, February 12, 2019, http://www.theengineer.co.uk/ai-medical-diagnostics.*

with the choice of database size, data format, and quality, this task becomes a subtle exercise that requires a lot of fine-tuning.

Another drawback is that artificial neural networks are subject to the phenomenon of overlearning. Contrary to what one might think, it is not enough to constantly increase the volume of data to indefinitely increase the accuracy. After a certain point, trying to further increase accuracy by adding data only increases confusion. The machine then becomes unable to process cases other than those by which it has already been trained.

For each change of context (for example, an additional regulation that changes a product's sale conditions), it is necessary to completely retrain the machine and regenerate a new version of the algorithm.

Artificial neural networks are like black boxes: you feed data into the machine, and it provides you results without you knowing how they were obtained. For some uses, this is exciting. For many uses, it's problematic.

Results are closer to trends than to exact results because this is a statistical approach. Accuracy varies between 70 and 95 percent. Thus, the detection of cancerous tumors on an X-ray system is far from comprehensive, as previously mentioned.

As with any statistical learning machine, an artificial neural network will produce classifications based on several specific categories initially given to it by its designer. It won't create any new categories while training.

To feed statistical learning machines, scientists have created three learning methods: supervised learning, unsupervised learning, and reinforcement learning.

The purpose of supervised learning is to train AI software algorithms to learn how to learn and to make data-based predictions. Training is therefore the key to obtaining the most reliable algorithm possible. If we take the example of an algorithm that recognizes faces, the user will have to define not only what a face is but also what it is not so that the algorithm can learn and predict if the next pictures are faces. The algorithm learns by example—or rather by examples. And this is the main difference it has with human beings: a child knows what a cat is after having seen two or three of them. Neural networks need to see thousands of cat pictures taken from all angles before reaching an acceptable level of results. In general, supervised learning is well suited when the data is structured (also referred to as labeled or tagged).

Unsupervised learning differs in that the system does not have annotated data from which to learn. It has only raw data without any classification examples done by humans. It must therefore learn on its own how to group together the data's various elements and to build different categories that were not defined at the outset. Today, the algorithms capable of assembling this data are called partitioning methods or clustering. They search for similarities and anomalies, but they do not make up category names. Data extraction is therefore descriptive (as opposed to predictive, as in supervised learning). For example, a program would be able to identify that one photo is of the countryside and another is of the mountains. It is often used in combination with supervised learning.

The two techniques described are interesting but leave room for many potential errors. Reinforcement learning is done through the process of iteration, so the machine memorizes that by carrying out action A under condition X, it will obtain a better score (often called a reward). Extensive effort is put into training the machine and noting its performance, though the scoring process can be automatic—for instance, based on a user satisfaction score online. This type of learning is often used to train chatbots on their dialogue performance.

Note that learning is a critical phase because AI alone does not invent knowledge. In our example of tumor detection in Beijing, discussed in chapter 5, the AI solution provider had indeed trained its neural network with labeled image databases that reflected radiologists' real knowledge. In a catastrophe version of a neural networks' statistical approach, the risk is the same as the follow-the-herd approach: if the first users of a neural system train the machine toward an error or false reasoning, the system will incite the following users to go in the same direction. Hence the importance of the system learning from quality data or the best experts in the field.

To set up a business solution based on machine learning, you need reliable and labeled data for the three phases of training, testing, and production. Even for unsupervised systems, you need tagged data in the first phase of learning. This means that your data must include a description of its nature.

The rules approach, as with statistical learning algorithms, needs input data. However, the data must be formally structured (for example, a CSV format). This technology makes it possible to automatically generate decision trees from the data. A decision tree is a diagram of criteria that will predict the output value based on the parameters of the input sample. For instance, to predict whether a patient has the flu, the criteria for this tree are the patient's recorded temperature and whether they are experiencing any vertigo or nausea symptoms. Once these criteria have been defined, you just need to test the values of the submitted sample to get the desired prediction. Each branch corresponds to one criterion, and each sheet corresponds to a possible category for the sample to be classified.

The great advantages of this technological approach include the following:

- The ability to open the "box" and trace the different criteria that led to the prediction. Workers can understand the elements that led to the decision.
- Training time is much less than what would be needed for an artificial neural network, which means a slightly better execution time if the decision tree is not too complex.
- The data is formal, which is a great advantage for textual data, ranges of values, or labels (but a major drawback for processing images or sound).

If a use case is complex, however, the decision tree can become huge. To solve this problem, different methods exist. The best known is the random forest algorithm.[32] When a rule maker builds a decision tree, its shape will be more or less random. That is, for the same prediction and for the same data set, the inductor

32 *There is some argument as to who developed the first random forest algorithm, but Leo Breiman and Adele Cutler registered random forests as a trademark in 2019.*

will never build the same tree. The random forest algorithm will therefore build a forest of decision trees all different but all geared to predict the same thing. It will sort these trees, choose the best, and cut the less relevant branches. In this way, without loss of precision, we obtain a smaller, faster, and more relevant tree, retaining the imperative of detecting the reasons underlying the data.

Rule drivers, or algorithms that produce decision trees (such as J48 or ID3),[33] coupled with the random forest algorithm, are a nice alternative to artificial neural networks. Choosing a business application built on this basis can be a good choice in terms of IT architecture.

You can now see that choosing the best self-learning solution to reach your goal is a matter for specialists. In the current state of offers, you need help to make the right architectural decisions, such as choosing the right AI platform and deploying it. Faced with the shortage of skills in this area, some pragmatic customers prefer to choose an alternative approach to neural networks, either a rules driver or a combination of the two technologies. Alternatively, they might move toward an expert systems solution, which is much easier to deploy but without any self-learning.

33 *This algorithm is a successor to ID3, developed by Quinlan Ross in 1993. It is also known as the J48 algorithm and is based on Hunt's algorithm.*

Reasoning on Data without Self-Learning

The goal of reasoning is to extract contextual knowledge from a data set to determine what actions to take or what the future trends will be. The first field of AI applications was reasoning with expert systems, which rely essentially on inference engine technology, a leading technology in today's AI space. Determinism, and therefore the accuracy of results, is the prime quality of inference engines. AI purists argue that this technology is pseudo-artificial intelligence because the system does not learn by itself and does not create reasoning algorithms. The rules are written by humans (computer scientists for the setup, then business experts for rule improvement) in charge of configuration. However, there is no decision tree written by hand, and the inference engine builds its reasoning logic by itself. Do note that this technology is well suited to applications of limited complexity (up to a few hundred rules maximum for performance reasons) and that its strength lies in explainable results. Millions of inference engines are successfully deployed worldwide, whether for autopilots in aircraft or medical and financial applications. Whenever the accuracy of the reasoning results is crucial, this technology should be considered.

Reasoning on data based on a deterministic approach is also complementary to self-learning based on statistical-type neural networks. Expert systems (or other rule engines) are geared toward the business process automation market that requires accuracy while machine and deep learning are more oriented toward uncovering trends, predictive and prescriptive analytics for which a margin of error is acceptable. Examples of deep learning uses are Netflix's recommendations based on a member's profile and history of movies seen, Facebook's advertising targeted to members based on the content of their posted messages and photos, and Amazon's product suggestions that complement purchases members have made. It is indeed your final application use (detection of trends or exact answer requirements) that will determine the best AI technology for your organization.

Human Language Processing

From the very beginning of computing, research centers all over the world have sought to meet the challenge of language processing, whether it be text or voice comprehension, natural language text generation (human language, for example, English), or, of course, intelligent dialogue defined by Alan Turing as the holy grail of AI tests (the famous 1950 Turing test). But the first application of language processing is undoubtedly automatic translation.

Automatic Translation

Early translation software, developed alongside the first computers, was based on rules and manually written dictionaries. In the 1990s, researchers created statistical methods: for each word, the computer calculated the most likely translation based on a body of references. Web page and document translation was sometimes approximate and literal (word for word), but early translation software offered basic content understanding without speaking the original language of the document and for a very low price. These tools were often used as first steps to help human translators slightly reduce their workload. Two important developments positively influenced machine translation results:

1. Software used increased computer power to move from word-to-word dictionaries to phrase-based machine translation (groups of nouns, verbs, and words). Through statistical analysis of documents translated by official bodies (such as international organizations' websites), dictionaries of sentences, words, and expressions are created and saved for reference. This method is effective but very expensive in computing power because each translated element requires a large calculation. Also, while it is possible to translate words and expressions without relying on rules, it becomes difficult to manage the order of sentences.

2. In 2014, machine translation started using neural networks. Rather than working sentence by sentence, neural networks create statistical models that are much less demanding of computing power. Each word is chosen based on probability using the entire original text and the sentence being translated to better estimate both the overall subject and the specific context of the sentence. This avoids false friends and allows a better consideration of the sentence structure.

Thanks to machine learning, translation tools were able to change paradigms and end the race toward the development of increasingly large dictionaries and ever more sophisticated calculations to create genuinely smarter algorithms. They translate better and use fewer resources.

The purpose of machine translation is to transform a text from one language to another. Translation software must be able to separate sentences and recognize subjects, verbs, and other linguistic elements. But it does not have to understand the meaning of the text as long as the conversion from one language to another is correct. This is where translation differs from natural language understanding.

Understanding Language

Today's communication between computers and human beings is still mostly done by a series of keystrokes and the click of a mouse or the touch of a finger on a screen. These interfaces create four major problems:

1. The user must learn how to use the software.
2. This interface is slow for many users, especially when using a keyboard.
3. The user must physically move near the computer to use it.
4. This interface is what we ironically called a bidirectional monologue (see chapter 3). It is always the user who asks a question or makes a request, and it

> is the machine that responds via the screen. There is no real dialogue as there is between two human beings who speak the same language and who both ask and answer questions.

NLU, or previously NLP, is the subdomain of AI that aims to understand human language. Though NLP is a term still used by some software companies, in reality the field of NLP covers a much wider spectrum in language processing.

NLU represents a very different technical challenge from translation, even though some original tools were based on similar technologies. The ultimate goal of NLU is to understand the meaning of a sentence, whether it is a question, an answer, a comment, a diagnosis, or a recommendation, in order to draw conclusions. Some NLU software tries to understand how a client talking about a company on social networks feels about it. Other software tries to automatically sort documents by subject (emails, for example) or understand a question so that it can be answered. NLU is thus an interface between human and machine that aims to go from computer searches by key words, such as *car purchase 15,000 dollars New York*, to a search including an action and a verb, such as *Siri, where can I buy a bike carrier tomorrow that is compatible with my Volkswagen car?*

The first linguistic comprehension and semantics solutions available at the end of the twentieth century were based on techniques where software counted the number of times a word or a polarity (positive or negative terms) appeared in the text to try to understand the meaning of a document. The addition of dictionaries (ontologies) allowed the computer to associate groups of words with ideas. For example, an article that contained the terms *fashion, leather goods, fine jewelry,* and *high fashion* was probably about luxury goods. Linguistic comprehension tools were based on many rules and dictionaries and were therefore neither particularly efficient nor particularly easy to maintain.

Today, with neural networks and new machine learning techniques, research has focused on unsupervised language learning. The computer itself creates the needed lexical fields and grammar rules without any body of reference processed upstream.

With AI and automatic self-learning, near-perfect voice recognition can be reached in laboratory conditions because of the power of servers and the availability of huge archive databases that include, among other things, tens of thousands of male and female voice samples. Understanding a voice, however, does not mean the virtual assistant understands the meaning of what is said.

Still, the percentage of correct answers is far from satisfactory, although Google Assistant's correct answer rate has increased by almost 20 percent in two years.[34] However, the four virtual assistants—Google Assistant, Apple's Siri, Microsoft's Cortana, and Amazon's Alexa—tested by Loup Ventures scored correct answers averaging 80 percent, with only Amazon showing real progress from the previous year. This demonstrates that actually

---

34 *Lauren Feiner, "Google's Assistant Is Still the Smartest, but Amazon's Alexa Is Getting Better Faster," CNBC Tech, updated August 16, 2019, http://www.cnbc.com/2019/08/16/google-assistant-beats-siri-and-alexa-in-iq-test-as-all-three-improve.html.*

understanding the meaning of a sentence or question is still NLU's weak area and is not improving as fast as other aspects of the technology.

Voice recognition is not that different from interpreting short written text. An additional component is needed to understand a verbal exchange: speech to text. This technology has been around for a while, though difficulties remain in interpreting the various users' native accents. The preliminary step is usually to turn the voice into text before analyzing it. If the exchanges are made with short sentences, without any argumentation or explanation, the results can be very interesting.

In the future, humans will be able to ask the computer a question or send an instruction verbally no matter where they are (at home, at the office, in their car), and the machine will take care of the rest, just like a real expert assistant would. Replacing the keyboard with voice input will give a significant advantage to companies with a simple name to pronounce or with a recognized brand. For example, verbally the user will be more likely to ask the price of a box of Kleenex than to use the generic term *tissue paper*.

To create a real user interface that does not require a keyboard and screen and allows sending instructions by voice, the computer must not only understand the language correctly but also be able to respond intelligently—that is to say without predefined scripted sentences. This ability to express itself is called natural language generation.

Language Generation—Text or Voice

Computer language generation has existed in a more or less primary form since the beginning of computing. Indeed, any time a warning message appears on a screen, the computer is transmitting it to the user in natural language (English, French, etc.). Important technical leaps have enabled computers to express increasingly complex ideas with more precision and nuance since the days when students were learning how to display the words *Hello, World!* on a screen.

There are three generations of language software available on the market:

1. The first generation, sentences with holes in them or templates, corresponds to predefined text completed by words or pieces of sentences during a database merge. These simple string operations are available with all basic computer languages and are used by business users, rather than IT specialists, to create contracts or email templates in office software, such as Microsoft Word, or to send marketing emails, thanks to such services as Mailchimp or marketing automation tools like HubSpot.

2. The second generation, NLG, is a template that conjugates. NLG entered the market in the 2000s, when software was developed that integrated a specific language's grammar rules. For example, NLG can automatically generate the sentences "Mr. Smith has opened a bank account" and "Mr. and Ms. Smith have

opened a bank account" from a single model. Indeed, the machine knows the grammar and thus the notions of tenses, subjects, verbs, objects, singular, plural, and all other necessary elements of a well-written text. NLG enabled the emergence of robo-journalism, with report models more flexible than gapped sentences that could generate millions of articles per year automatically. This was mainly used to produce comments in areas with low-volume data (stock market reports, earthquake alerts, scores, and game results).

3. The third generation of NLG develops an outline before writing the text. Since the mid-2010s, this smarter new generation is gaining traction, in particular with the ability to summarize data. Rather than generating a text point by point (a gap equals a variable), the software analyzes the data, automatically decides what is important based on calculations and reasoning (it writes a plan), then generates text from the results of this analysis. No longer starting from a template but from a plan described in key words or intentions, and given more freedom of writing, the tool can now produce an exponentially increased volume of texts (and variations). This is one of the significant results of third-generation NLG. It then becomes necessary and critical to provide feedback to the NLG tool to help it choose between all the sentences by checking them against established grammar rules.

In the future, to meet this new challenge, NLG will be paired with other techniques, such as machine learning, to learn from users' comments.

It should be noted that text generation, or natural language generation, has practically nothing in common with natural language understanding. NLU tries to understand unstructured data (text or voice), whereas NLG reasons from structured data that has meaning and is usually stored in a database. For example, you analyze a client's known data in your CRM software, which will summarize their relationship with your company in four or five sentences. To fully understand this market, it is necessary to analyze the four types of text a human being produces that NLG software must be able to generate:

1. Comments
2. Situation summaries
3. Analysis
4. Reasoned recommendations

Natural Language Generation (NLG) Software Can Generate Four Types of Text Depending on Its Development Level

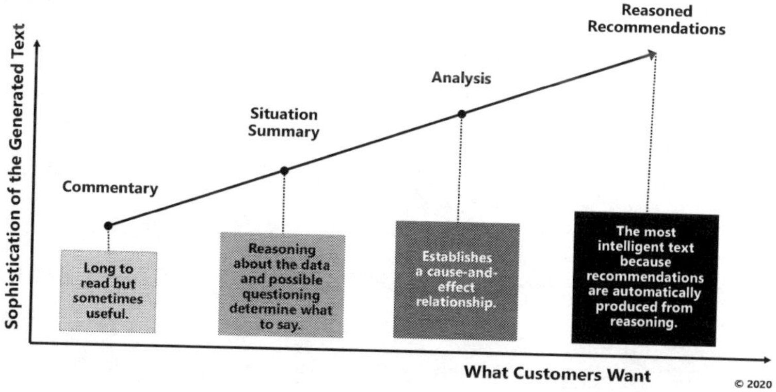

Generating a comment is relatively easy. You just need to analyze the data and fill in gapped sentences, replacing variables with real data. For instance, consider the generic phrase *This customer's last order dates to DD MM 20YY and amounts to $$$$ of sales revenue for products XXX and YYY*. You just need to replace the variables *DD, MM, YY, $$$$, XXX,* and *YYY* with values from a client database to get a coherent sentence that adapts to each client's situation. This example is a particularly simple one. If, for example, there are three products instead of two, you would include the coordinating conjunction *and* before the last product listed: *for products XXX, YYY, and ZZZ*. With limited volumes, comments can be simply managed with gapped sentences. In the most common uses, online descriptions of products and services are in the form of commentaries.

Generating a situation summary is a little more complicated because it requires a data analysis tool. To produce a summary, it is necessary to determine what important information must be included and what useless information must be eliminated. You must therefore work upstream with an organization's business experts to set thresholds and value weights for the key data. For example, a 5 percent merchandise inventory change may be low-interest information, whereas a 1.5 percent margin increase is significant information. In addition, experience shows that the content of the summary depends on the reader, who will need to be questioned about their priorities. All data is not of equal importance, depending on each reader and their individual role in the company. Let's note that writing a summary is not as simple as writing a comment because this job requires reasoning on available data, and a dedicated tool is needed.

Writing analysis-type text raises the level of difficulty when compared to both commentaries and summaries, but readers like it because it explains causes. Writing an analysis or a diagnosis not only requires reasoning on data but also determining rules derived from your business logic. Experience shows that it takes an expert only a few days' work to define the rules and exceptions that are this knowledge base's foundation. It must be technically independent from the intended end use (web, client mailings, technical team assistance, frequently asked questions, chatbots, etc.) because it can have multiple uses. In addition to this design work, you'll need to allow a few weeks of configuration and testing to validate the overall coherence. In a nutshell, with an automated analysis solution, you are taking the first step toward industrializing your expertise. This is a strategic topic for your company because your competitors may still be unaware that this collaborative AI choice is even possible.

Finally, knowing how to write recommendations-type text along with a contextual individualized argumentation for each customer sets up an individualized advice production tool of remarkable efficiency with zero marginal cost. An initial example of use was given in chapter 4, scenario 6. Here is another one in the context of a hardware store:

Upon receipt of your information on our website, it seems that your wall is made of hollow blocks and covered with plaster. This construction type is really too fragile to support your kitchen appliances on its own. I therefore recommend that you use these new XYZ store reference toggle fasteners, which are perfectly adapted to this particular context and which are available in stock at the store located 1.7 miles from you at XXX address.

Toggle fasteners will allow you to hang your appliances up to a load of fifty pounds per fastener, despite the weakness of the brick. It is the ideal product for you!

Studies have shown that knowing how to explain to a prospect why a product or service is well suited to their needs greatly increases the conversion rate. HubSpot found that a personalized call-to-action button performed 202 percent better than a standard one.[35] Moreover, customers are fond of this type of text because it is intellectually rich and explains the best solution, educating the reader or the web user in the process. If you educate your customers on your products, then you become a market leader.

Generating voice rather than text requires two changes: First, it requires the addition of a text-to-speech tool (an inverse function of speech to text). There is a wide availability of choices and of voices. Second, it requires the generated text (which will then be converted into voice) to be of high quality. Indeed, if the text generator has omitted a comma in a written document, the reader's brain will automatically add it without any consequences. In a verbal translation, however, the lack of a comma may cause the writing to become incomprehensible.

Finally, it is important to remember that such an integration into a company's information system relies on the ever-growing need to produce rich text and therefore suggests data access standardization. A NLG system for communicating with humans must first be able to access the data needed to generate text.

---

35 *Jeffrey Vocell, "Personalized Calls to Action Perform 202% Better Than Basic CTAs," HubSpot, updated January 29, 2018, https://blog.hubspot.com/marketing/personalized-calls-to-action-convert-better-data#sm.000awoxgniktcoi11jl2et1nit4os.*

Dialogue

In most cases, dialogue requires not only understanding questions but also reasoning in order to construct intelligent answers in natural language. Of course, if a dialogue is about searching for such information as tomorrow's weather, the reasoning phase is not necessary. But if, for instance, the question is to find an order's delivery date, it is essential not only to access the database that contains the order and available stock information but also to calculate the delivery time according to the customer's address. If the dialogue is used in a commercial context, justifying why the proposed product is well suited to a prospect's needs requires reasoning that explains the cause-and-effect relationship.

Thanks to technical progress, computers have gone from machines capable of receiving, calculating, storing, and transmitting results to AIs capable of responding to human vocal commands. Soon they will be able to explain situations. The human-computer relationship is growing both as machines become smarter and as human language becomes the natural exchange interface with computers. At the January 2019 Consumer Electronics Show in Las Vegas, Amazon's Alexa software demonstrated its technical superiority in speech understanding and a slew of Alexa-enabled products were unveiled, solidifying Alexa as the market leader. As CNET put it, "if electricity runs through it [a device], it can work with the Alexa voice assistant."[36]

---

36 *Ben Fox Rubin and Ry Crist, "What Amazon's Alexa will tell us in 2019," CNET Smart Home, January 18, 2019, http://www.cnet.com/news/what-amazon-alexa-will-tell-us-in-2019.*

Visual Recognition

We have briefly touched on visual recognition while discussing machine learning and, more specifically, deep learning. Visual recognition that automatically recognizes videos and images is one of AI's most mature technologies. Neural network technology lends itself particularly well to this use and supports learning by analogy. Therefore, we have two steps: image analysis and content recognition. Recognizing the content of an image is the most interesting because it allows many applications, such as intelligent monitoring of a place, identifying products in a supermarket cart to bypass the checkout register, or even sorting waste. How does content recognition work? Not surprisingly, it is based on deep learning.

You have the choice between two types of learning methods: supervised and unsupervised classification of images. The easiest approach to teach a self-driving car road traffic regulation signs is to have humans teach the software. Each panel is labeled and the technical team helps the car's software make the link between a stop sign and the vehicle stopping at that sign. This is called supervised learning. On the other hand, unsupervised image classification is chosen for detecting unknown objects. In the case of a self-driving car, you would choose this type of detection for objects that are moving on the road, some of which may be unlisted ones. For example, the real case of a duck flying across the road would prompt a necessary decision to brake or not depending on the duck's distance, its height above the ground, and its flight speed.

Visual recognition, whatever the chosen technology, will have an influence on different aspects of our daily life. For example, for a smoother flow in cafeteria lines, the dishes you put on your tray can be identified instantaneously at checkout before you pay.

On the other hand, facial recognition is still somewhat unreliable. In July 2018, the American Civil Liberties Union tested Amazon's famous *Rekognition* software. The software mistakenly identified twenty-eight members of the US Congress as having a serious criminal record and having already been arrested for a felony.[37] The system had been trained with thousands of photos of every congressman and congresswoman to achieve this statistic, however imperfect. No significant progress was made in 2019. In any case, such a statistical technology does not achieve accuracy. It is clear that a human being needs to double-check the results. This is why collaborative AI is the future of this industry. Lastly, the Chinese government's claim that it can recognize every pedestrian in a city automatically leaves many serious AI experts skeptical and flabbergasted.

Augmented reality, which adds virtual elements to a concrete situation (for example, overlaying clothing on your photo, as seen in chapter 3), is a different market from visual recognition and is not considered part of AI. However, with AI it is possible to go beyond image recognition. There are image transformation applications available today that enable video and image editing. You can change the color of wallpaper on an image, turn a running horse into a zebra on a video, and

37 *Jacob Snow, "Amazon's Face Recognition Falsely Matched 28 Members of Congress with Mugshots," ACLU Free Future, July 26, 2018, http://www.aclu.org/blog/privacy-technology/surveillance-technologies/amazons-face-recognition-falsely-matched-28.*

erase a person or a plane in the sky on a photo. All these editing applications are now very functional.

AI Decision-Making

Many experts believe that relying on artificial neural networks to make decisions is bound to involve real legal, qualitative, and customer satisfaction risks. Indeed, the statistical approach inevitably leads to an error rate. Again, there are two possible choices that can be combined:

1. You can use an expert system based on an inference engine with a deterministic reasoning mode (like an Excel spreadsheet with formulas you define). Any responsibility for errors is easily attributable to whoever wrote the rules, but errors are easily corrected, as would be the case if your estimated budget on Excel was wrong because of a formula error. If you test your application correctly, however, there is no reason to get an unreliable final application.
2. You can use a neural network with a statistical mode of reasoning, and you'll know that by definition, the error rate will vary between 5 and 30 percent. In this case, the responsibility lies with whoever made the decision to use a statistical-type technology to do something other than what a neural network is designed for, to discover trends and processes.

Anytime you use a neural network in decision-making, you should note that the results will not necessarily be correct. In the case of Facebook using AI solutions to display targeted advertising to its members, an error rate of even a few tenths of a percent is perfectly acceptable. Indeed, the relevance rate of the ads would probably have been less than 5 percent without AI (deep learning in their case), but no one will get hurt by an out-of-context and poorly targeted advertisement.

For now, our basic advice for any AI project is to clearly separate the use cases: for risky projects, where a deterministic approach is essential because answers must always be accurate; and those for which an error rate is acceptable, knowing that it is most often inferior to that generated by human beings in the context of a repetitive task. In the first case, you would choose an expert system (inference engine) or write an application with a traditional decision tree configuration. In the other case, a neural network statistical choice is a good choice. Again, it is not uncommon to see one part of the prediction being done with a decision tree and the other with a deep learning–based application (or neural network).

This chapter gave you some technical knowledge about AI that is available to date. AI is not magic. Yet, its importance is considerable: all business applications in use (CRM, ERP, etc.) are being rewritten to include AI components. That is why it is so important for business owners and their executive committees to acquire basic AI knowledge. In addition, it is now crucial to understand the potential of collaborative AI, especially as financial barriers continue to fall and AI technologies become increasingly accessible. There are no more excuses: every business needs to focus on AI to augment their employees.

8.

The Future of Artificial Intelligence Technology

As machines get more intelligent and can better adapt to their users, people may end up preferring [to deal] with machines [rather] than with people.

Hector Geffner[38]

38 *Hector Geffner is a researcher at Pompeu Fabra University in Barcelona, Spain.*

The years 2018 & 2019 will probably be remembered as AI's coming of age. AI is maturing into a field aware of its limitations and actively pursuing targeted growth. These three sample events show just why:

1. The Defense Advanced Research Projects Agency (DARPA), the Pentagon's strategic innovation funding agency, invested in explainable artificial intelligence (XAI), thereby partially challenging neural networks, machine learning's core technology, and openly criticizing its black-box aspect and its statistical approach. XAI is built around the idea that AI systems must be able to explain their reasoning process.[39]

2. One of the most recognized global companies that had relied on AI to rebound lost one of its most important global contracts, despite that AI was supposed to have revolutionized its medical research.[40]

---

39 *"DARPA to Invest $2bn to Accelerate Third Wave of AI Programmes," Army Technology, September 11, 2018, http://www.army-technology.com/news/darpa-invest-2bn-artificial-intelligence.*

40 *Unfortunately, we are unable to share names here because our knowledge comes from the end customer and is covered by nondisclosure agreements. We can say that this medical project was supposed to be one of the biggest AI projects in the field, and it failed because the machine learning aspect of the AI could not do what the company had promised it would do.*

3. For what Elon Musk called security reasons, he released (as open source) his AI-based self-driving software. Was he really admitting his inability to find a reliable technological solution?

What's going on? What does the future hold? Describing the future of AI is a treacherous exercise because AI solution providers feed the press too many marketing messages that are neither validated by facts nor, above all, by credible success stories. Rather than enter into a futuristic science fiction debate, what follows are five short- and medium-term hypotheses (not use cases) on the technological progress of AI. These hypotheses are predictions ranked in order of importance and based on our years of work in the AI space, but they are by no means certainties.

The Future of Machine Learning

As a premise throughout this book, we believe that the goal of equipping computers with software that can automatically learn from company data and generate powerful computer programs without any human intervention is a revolutionary concept. To illustrate this point, we predict it is likely that such companies as Google or Facebook will offer, in the medium term, customized CRMs automatically generated from their AI platforms. These will reason on your prospects' data to generate a CRM dedicated to the company's marketing development. Google already knows better than any business just how and with which key words prospects find each website. They will likely apply the same business model as Booking.com or Hotels.com, which charges a commission on hotel room sales made on their platforms.

The US government seems to have understood the risk that AI-based GAFA dominance would represent, potentially turning every company in the world into a franchise spin-off. DARPA is the well-known American agency for advanced research projects to which we owe, among other things, the financing of COBOL language development and the internet. It clearly states on its website and in its publications that machine learning solutions based on neural networks are opaque, nonintuitive, and difficult to understand. In July 2018, the agency formalized its decision to fund a $2 billion project for self-learning software components that would offset the previously mentioned drawbacks. They might also be aiming to stop GAFA's empirical development.

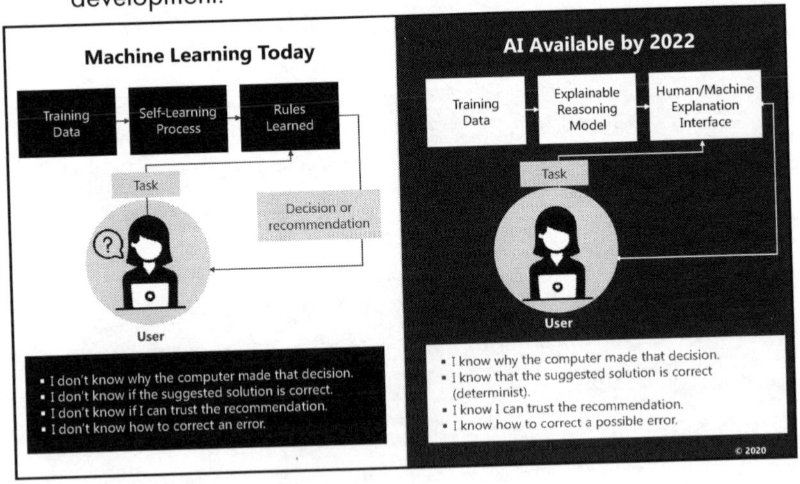

XAI is the new approach of AI. Eleven universities and private organizations are working on this subject, and the first prototypes were delivered in 2019. A production version won't be available for another eighteen to thirty-six months, but the resources deployed are commensurate with the objectives.

The goal of XAI is to provide a range of self-learning tools that not only explain their reasoning logic but also rationalize and predict their future behavior and the decisions they will make. Logically, a user might wonder why they should trust answers provided by a self-learning algorithm. XAI will not only answer that but also explain how the answers were obtained. This deterministic approach is what computer science has always been about, and that's why users trust the software they use. Understanding how a result has been reached will also allow people to improve self-learning algorithms. Even if it is too early to detail how XAI works, one can imagine that this third generation of AI will be a mixed bag, combining a deterministic system of handwritten, rules-based inference engines (expert systems) with the relatively newer AI-based self-learning approach founded on neural networks. In the end, it will be easier to regulate an understandable platform that can be audited than it is to regulate a neural network's black box.

The Three Generations of AI Reasoning

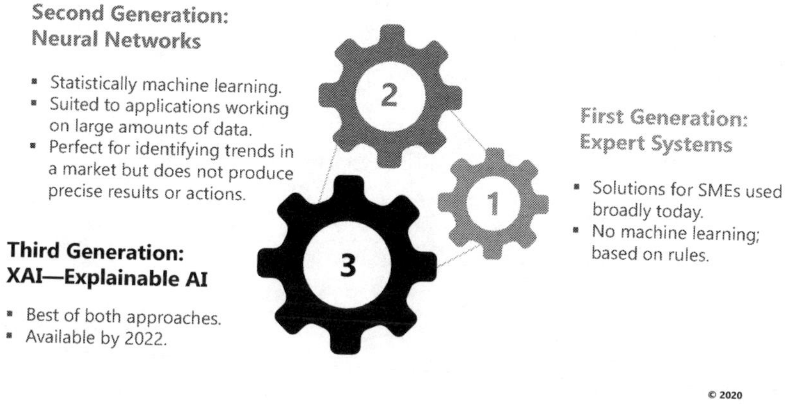

With XAI, fears of machines going off the deep end and controlling the world are relegated to science fiction. Instead, looking forward we can conclude that year zero of computer self-learning at a large scale is almost here!

The Future of Language Processing

As mentioned throughout this book, language processing has made tremendous progress, and yet there is still significant room for improvement in three main areas:

Understanding the meaning of a text (or an oral dialogue) beyond a simple sentence. Many scientific laboratories and start-ups are working on this matter because the potential market is huge but so is the technological challenge involved.

Developing more intelligent dialogue solutions that would be able to understand the meaning of a question in a more efficient way than they do today. This would also often require reasoning on existing data to produce intelligent questions and to go beyond a script of predefined answers.

Progressing in the generation of arguments, where software will explain a cause-and-effect relationship in natural language without manual programming.

The next few years should provide some interesting solutions in this fundamental area of language processing.

The Rise of the AI Agency

In 2018 & 2019, many large consulting agencies described the AI services market as one of the fastest growing market segments, with annual growth in excess of 100 percent but many clients are still looking for the applicable scenarios. Throughout this book, we have discussed many use cases of AI, and almost every use case has required more than one AI technology and a collaborative approach between humans and AI. This means that there is no one-stop shop for AI solutions. Despite what some AI vendors say, most successful AI projects will require a collaborative approach and multiple AI technologies. Meanwhile, many AI companies see all other AI companies as competitors and aren't necessarily interested in working together. How can you, as a business, navigate this potential minefield to use the right mix of technologies and not have to build your own (expensive) in-house team of AI experts?

The world of marketing provides us with a perfect example. As a marketer, you could buy marketing automation software, write all the rules, buy website content management system software, build the site, run advertisements, and so on. However, most companies don't do this. Instead, they hire a marketing agency of experts who know the software and know their business. These experts choose the best-of-breed software, build the marketing road map, and implement the solutions. Companies use marketing agencies to help them succeed with marketing technology, and soon companies will use AI agencies to help them succeed with collaborative AI projects.

The AI agency you hire for your business will have expertise both in AI software and in your line of business. It will audit your business to understand where AI might disrupt your business or where it might help you scale and increase margins. Then the agency will build an AI road map recommending the right mix of software to solve specific problems in your business. It will then oversee the implementation of the AI projects and partner with you in the long term to develop and implement a long-term AI strategy.

The Future of Personal AI

We also predict that alternatives to GAFA servers and collected data could surface. These servers manage not only data but also machine learning platform processing. Given the series of scandals over some of GAFA's collection and use of data, several initiatives are being implemented to offer personal or internal AI solutions to companies. In the same way that we manage separate personal and professional email accounts, we could have our own AI-dedicated file storage service, which would collect not only our personal data but also the rules of our personal AI applications. Each user could, or not, grant other external applications access to their data or even share their own AI-based applications. For example, we could allow our physician access to our medical data only and allow our favorite clothing store access to our measurements and previous purchase information so that it can suggest a more relevant selection of items.

The inventor of the World Wide Web, Sir Tim Berners-Lee, announced an initiative that goes in this direction with a project called Solid, taking place at MIT. This project and other similar ones could provoke a craze as soon as XAI becomes available. This movement will probably take a few years to become a global trend.

The Future of Connected Objects

Connected objects are not, by definition, artificial intelligence, but if we consider that data is the cornerstone of today's and tomorrow's AI, then the technological advances of these dispersed sensors are fundamental to the future of AI. Indeed, human beings make too many mistakes when they collect data manually. Entering information on a keyboard is not a contemporary industrial approach. The only current alternative is to use connected objects (sensors connected to the internet) as long as they are correctly installed. The current progress being made is directed toward miniaturizing sensors (some will be the size of a grain of rice) but also toward improving their technical quality (for instance, very high-definition miniature cameras). Finally, dedicated networks that transport impressive amounts of data collected by sensors continue to make amazing progress.

The future of AI will be based on automatic data collection, which is why it may be necessary for the United States to legislate the processing and storage of data, just as Europe has started to do.

The Future and the Unknown

To finish this chapter, let's point out a few things about the unknown. Simple AI, the limited AI mentioned in chapter 2, is available today but is monodisciplinary. Therefore, it cannot be creative, have common sense or empathy, or improve its knowledge by learning from experience, as humans do. The following graphic shows the evolution that we dream about, but no one really knows when, or if, it will ever become a reality. AGI would solve what simple AI cannot. Its multidisciplinary learning capability would allow for considerable progress because it could learn from the different subject areas studied by the machine. For example, by learning one hundred different languages, it could automatically detect any inconsistencies and suggest logical changes in each language. AI would then be creative and could propose a new simple language that would synthesize all existing languages by following a rigorous logic. Its common sense would allow it to reject nonlogical human suggestions. Finally, superintelligent AI might have a conscience that could lead to the domination of the human species or, conversely, that could understand the importance of certain values necessary to the harmonious development of relations between humans. But that is really crossing over into science fiction.

The Three Types of Artificial Intelligence

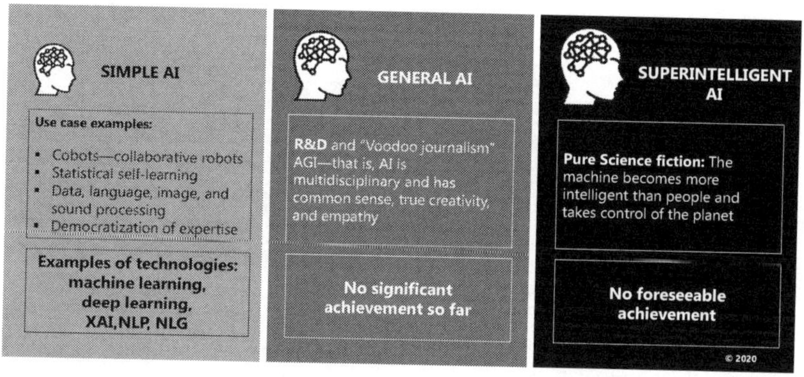

Conclusion

We have discussed how artificial intelligence will transform service sector companies, whether their activities are related to B2B or B2C services. We have seen that those who think of using AI to automate everything and replace employees are probably wrong. The AI revolution is mainly based on three components that we have illustrated throughout this book:

1. The automation of some repetitive tasks so that employees are free to focus on value-added tasks or automation, with the ultimate goal of promoting new services that would be prohibitively expensive to sell if produced manually.
2. The ability to augment knowledge workers with cobots to help them be more efficient and to make better decisions while also reducing their stress.
3. The premium repositioning of your business thanks to collaborative AI. AI is indeed crucial for digitizing individualized expertise and making the product easy to buy and use, for generalizing one-to-one marketing that explains the added value of a product or service to customers in an individualized way, and for industrializing the production of truly custom-made services for each customer.

Today, there are two types of service companies: those that will adopt collaborative AI for their core business and those that will disappear. In industrial production, many companies that did not automate part of their assembly lines before the year 2000 no longer exist. Those that tried to replace employees have learned that they actually need them for many tasks. It is up to service activities to industrialize their core business and to offer their customers excellent and better services without any significant effect on prices. Tomorrow, and even today, collaborative AI is essential. Companies that do not soon embrace AI are doomed to failure.

Throughout this book, we have discussed the major changes that collaborative AI will bring to your businesses. Collaborative AI will also improve human relations if it is correctly used. It may be a bit scary for experts to consider delegating their power, but it will lead to a new era of tremendous growth where soft skills, willpower, and respect for customers will prevail over knowledge and experience, thus building confidence.

As we have seen, collaborative AI will change the nature of our jobs. We believe, as John F. Kennedy said, that "a rising tide lifts all boats," and so this new AI approach should better our society as a whole. To achieve this, it is necessary to promote collaborative AI in every company so that it serves and benefits all. It is up to everyone to be aware of this and to act accordingly.

Now is the time for you to take action. To help you, we have created cobot-ai.com, where you will find practical advice and where you can contact us to book a conference on AI for your executive committee. You can also find all our articles on the subject on each of our LinkedIn profiles:

John Rauscher: http://www.linkedin.com/in/j-rauscher | Website: cobot-ai.com

Matt Rauscher: http://www.linkedin.com/in/mattrauscher | Website: nituno.com

Abbreviations

AGI	artificial general intelligence
AI	artificial intelligence
AR	augmented reality
BI	business intelligence
B2B	business-to-business
B2C	business-to-consumer
Cobots	collaborative robots
CRM	customer relationship management
DARPA	Defense Advanced Research Projects Agency
ERP	enterprise resource planning
GAFA	Google, Amazon, Facebook, and Apple
GDP	gross domestic product
GDPR	General Data Protection Regulation
IoT	Internet of things
IT	information technology
ML	machine learning
MVP	minimum viable (and virtuous) product
NLG	natural language generation
NLP	natural language processing
NLU	natural language understanding
R&D	research and development
ROI	return on investment
RPA	robot processing automation
SEA	search engine advertising
SEO	search engine optimization
SME	small-to-medium enterprise
VR	virtual reality
XAI	explainable artificial intelligence

Glossary of Useful AI Terms for Setting Up Collaborative AI

In the following glossary, the term *computer* includes AI algorithms, so it includes software as well. These descriptions are deliberately simplified to be easily understood by the general public.

computer vision, artificial vision: The field of artificial intelligence that aims to teach computers how to imitate human vision and interpret what is seen.

deep learning: An approach to computer-based machine learning using a technology called artificial neural networks. In the context of deep learning, neural networks connect to multiple layers of neurons to obtain more accurate summary results. They also require more data and a longer training phase.

expert systems, rule engines, inference engines: First-generation AI software that does not include a self-learning function. Rules are handwritten, but the system automatically creates a decision tree. The maintenance of a reasoning algorithm is thus greatly simplified.

explainable AI (XAI): Third-generation AI under development as of 2019 that aims to solve the black-box effect related to learning by neural networks. With XAI, humans will be able to understand how the computer builds its machine learning algorithms and how it achieves the results it produces.

machine learning (ML): Software that learns automatically by working toward a human-defined goal based on observed trends in the data for the purpose of producing an algorithm; a program created without human intervention.

natural language generation (NLG): A subdomain of NLP, NLG aims to generate text and voice from reasoning supported by data. Indeed, when one speaks and one writes, that is expressing one's reasoning in natural language. This reasoning is based on rules (business or cultural) applied to a context (the data).

natural language processing (NLP): The field of artificial intelligence that aims to automate exchanges in natural language, such as English or French, between computers and human beings. This area of AI includes language recognition, language generation, and intelligent dialogue, in both oral and written forms.

natural language understanding (NLU): A subdomain of NLP, NLU aims to understand text and voice and, to a certain extent, the meaning of what is read or heard.

reinforcement learning: An approach to machine learning in which computers learn to perform a task just like a child would, with an automatic scoring system that awards good or bad points depending on the result. The goal is for the system to improve on its own by attempting different combinations.

robot processing automation (RPA): The use of software with, most of the time, AI algorithms to automate repetitive tasks that previously required humans to perform.

supervised learning: A learning technique in which the computer learns to solve a specific task using data organized and annotated by human supervisors to make it easier to understand, such as an Excel spreadsheet with well-specified columns. It is used to detect spam, fraud, or even weather forecasts based on known scenarios.

unsupervised learning: An approach to machine learning with bulk data. It is up to the computer to find the patterns of data and behaviors on its own.

weak or simple AI: The artificial intelligence available in 2019. AI that can do only one thing at a time, whether it is to win the game of Go or chess or to recognize a specific object. In no case does the computer have its own conscience, common sense, judgmental ability, or true creativity. The dream of artificial intelligence labs is to reach the next stage known as artificial general intelligence (AGI), which would provide multidisciplinary self-learning computers.

Made in the USA
Monee, IL
05 November 2026

68020978R00127